PRAISE FOR MIDNIGHTS

"There is almost no writer I admire as much as I do Alec Wilkinson. He's an extraordinary reporter and a writer of such grace that his stories seem illuminated from within. His work has enduring brilliance and humanity."
—SUSAN ORLEAN, author of *On Animals*

"*Midnights* is a generous slice of small-town Americana written in clear and gorgeous prose by a narrator we can all identify with. Wilkinson is the perfect guide for the murky and often hilarious world of a rural police department. As a young writer, I used this book as an example of what to emulate and what to aspire to."
—SEBASTIAN JUNGER, author of *Freedom*

"*Midnights* vividly clarifies both the boredom and the moments of sheer terror, the humorous incidents, camaraderie and frustration of being a police officer in an area where nothing supposedly happens."
—*GQ*

"*Midnights* is both a comedy of errors and an affectionate portrait."
—*Time*

"This is a superb work of repor'' ''

T0007710

MIDNIGHTS

MIDNIGHTS

A YEAR WITH
THE WELLFLEET POLICE

Alec Wilkinson

FOREWORD BY WILLIAM MAXWELL
AFTERWORD BY THE AUTHOR

BOSTON

GODINE NONPAREIL

2023

Published in 2023 by
GODINE
Boston, Massachusetts
godine.com

LIBRARY OF CONGRESS CATALOGING-IN-PUBLICATION DATA
Names: Wilkinson, Alec, 1952- author.
Title: Midnights : a year with the Wellfleet police / Alec Wilkinson ;
    foreword by William Maxwell ; afterword by the author.
Description: Boston : Godine, 2023. | Originally published in 1982
    by Random House.
Identifiers: LCCN 2022016816 (print) | LCCN 2022016817 (ebook) |
    ISBN 9781567927504 (paperback) | ISBN 9781567927511 (ebook)
Subjects: LCSH: Police--Massachusetts--Wellfleet.
Classification: LCC HV8148.W36 W54 2023 (print)
    | LCC HV8148.W36 (ebook)
    | DDC 363.209744/92--dc23/eng/20220609
LC record available at https://lccn.loc.gov/2022016816
LC ebook record available at https://lccn.loc.gov/2022016817

First Printing, 2023
Printed in the United States of America

This book is for
Celia Owens
and
William Maxwell

The experiences described in this book are from nearly half a century ago. Here and there are language and attitudes that are no longer appropriate, but I thought that to amend them would be dishonest and to make myself out to be an unreliable witness.

CONTENTS

Foreword

I CANNOT PRETEND that I have no personal interest in the author of this book. Or in the book itself. I rode to the train station with Alec Wilkinson's father, in his jeep, from a country road in northern Westchester for I have lost track of how many years. In his basement workshop he had every tool I was ever likely to need, and he could fix anything. When he moved to Wellfleet, on Cape Cod, I didn't see how I would ever manage without him.

My first recollection of Alec, though I must have seen him many times before this, is of a little boy writing hieroglyphs on the evening air with a Fourth of July sparkler. Then of an ominous silence upstairs at the Wilkinsons': in order to avoid hitting a child who ran in front of his bicycle, Alec had braked too suddenly, was catapulted over the handlebars, and landed on his head. Then I sit in the Wilkinsons' living room listening politely to Alec's four-piece string band. I am of the wrong generation for rock music and prefer to be somewhere else when it is going on. Then I am at a concert he gave—by now he is a young man just out of Bennington College—on the flattop guitar in the Congregational Church in Wellfleet. This time I don't wish I were somewhere else, but I am struck not only by the fact that Alec plays extremely well but also by his easy, natural manner on the platform. Then, wearing a policeman's uniform, he is going the rounds of stores and restaurants in Wellfleet at night, making sure they haven't been broken into. And finally, he and I are sitting at a folding card table on the grass in front of the Packing Box House.

We—my wife and younger daughter and I—had been staying in a lovely old saltbox deep in the woods that was available only out of season, and at the beginning of July we weren't ready to leave the ocean. "There's a house," Alec's father said. "It's on Gull Pond. But you wouldn't like it. It belongs to a man who worked for the telephone company. I hear the house is partly made of scrap lumber. What they used to ship those glass insulators in and miles of telephone wire. If you'd said earlier that you wanted something . . ." But Alec drove over and walked around the outside of the house and said, "I think you might want to look at it." There was nothing else and so we took it.

The owner was living in Germany and had put the house in the hands of elderly relatives, who rented it for him in summer but also used it as a repository for unwanted furniture. It was not an ordinary house, in any case. The front door opened on the toilet. After we had filled one bedroom with chests of drawers, end tables, ugly bridge lamps, and uncomfortable dining room chairs, not to mention a prehistoric sewing machine and a Victrola whose cartridge and needle had been eaten by rust, it became possible to move from room to room—in places just barely. But the windows of one side of the house looked out on the pond, and there was a glassed-in porch, where we sat at one of the two dining room tables. My wife, with a box of Windsor and Newton watercolors and a glass of murky water that she dipped her brushes into, painted still lifes of summer wildflowers or the interior of the house, and I read and wrote letters. No car or truck ever drove by. The only sound from the outdoors in the daytime was the call of the local bobwhite and after dark the owl and whippoorwill. In spite of the inconveniences, we were quite happy there. One day my daughter said, "Father, Alec is writing a book and he wondered if you would read a little of it."

I read a few pages and see that the material is fresh and the writing is not at all bad. In fact, it is quite good in places. I read on. The next afternoon we are sitting at the card table again. I read and then we talk and then I read some more. Alec is a quick study. I need only to demonstrate once that most adjectives and adverbs are unnecessary, and that style in writing comes from an awareness on the writer's part of his own habitual patterns of speech. "Would it work better," I say, "to move this paragraph to the bottom of the next page?" and "This incident may be just a little too much like something in the previous chapter and should possibly be cut." and

"This is nice. What about expanding it into a chapter by itself?" It is how I have made my living for the past forty years. Fiddling with words.

Day after day we sit there. My wife brings glasses of iced tea. Or we consider the snake hole I have discovered out by the road. Then we sit down again and I say, "Since you have handled the monologue form successfully with the chief (bob bob-*white*!), what about trying it again with some of the others?" If it is too hot to think, we give up and go swimming. And the book grows longer and longer.

At the end of the month we pack up our things and drive home. We might have rented the Packing Box House for the following summer except that someone in the family that had it after us sent a baseball through one of the windows in the glassed-in porch, and instead of replacing the broken glass, the caretakers boarded it over. Also, they were seen taking more furniture into the house.

That winter Alec drove down at regular intervals from his brother's house on the Hudson and we went on working, only now it was in front of the fireplace, with snow deep on the ground outside. He had learned anything I had to teach him and I think it was merely the desire to have some response to what he had written that made him keep coming.

REREADING THE BOOK after nearly twenty years I am happy to find it is even better than I remembered it as being. The style is simple and direct, and because Alec is a trained musician he has an ear for odd and revealing turns of speech. Also, how visual it is. The reader is presented not only with the look—mostly nighttime since he was on duty between 8 P.M. and 4 A.M.—but the whole life of a small New England summer resort, in and out of season. The eight uniformed men who figure in the narrative are given room to breathe, to be candid, to be themselves. How human they are, and much of the time how forlorn. Ill-paid, obliged to keep different hours from their families, estranged from their friends, sassed with impunity by adolescent punks, at the mercy of the town's selectmen. But also how good-natured they are—training a rookie (the author) that they know will only be on the force a year, they show him how to treat a pistol with proper respect, how to diffuse quarrels between husbands and wives, where it is safe to park the police car and grab forty winks when he is overcome by the desire for sleep, how to deal with suicides and autopsies. They are ordinary men, but they are also heroes. Pressing the gas pedal all the way to the floor, they take off down Route 6 after a speeding car that may only be an overexcited kid or a sociopath with a gun and a grievance against cops.

William Maxwell,
2000

MIDNIGHTS

THE WELLFLEET POLICE DEPARTMENT (1975-76)

Richard Huntley (the chief)

Gary Joseph (the sergeant)

Billy Brooks

Paul Francis

Sherman A. Merrill, Jr.

Chickie Berrio

Charlie Valli

Joe Hogan

1.

In May of 1975, when I was twenty-three years old, five months out of college, with a degree in music, and without any idea of what to do with myself, I took a job as a policeman in Wellfleet, Massachusetts, and resolved to stay with it for a year because I thought it would do me good. I was lonely much of the time, as well as scared, surprised, excited, embarrassed, self-righteous, and many other things, too. I spent hours at a stretch hoping nothing serious would happen when I was working alone; I never quite shook the feeling that I was a fraud; and on several occasions, when it all seemed to be too much, I meant to quit, but I never did.

Wellfleet is near the end of Cape Cod. My parents built a summer house there thirty years ago, and I have spent a lot of time in it and on the beaches and in the woods around it. I feel at home in Wellfleet. It has a number of memories for me. It restores me whenever I visit it. Out of affection for the place I like to say I grew up there, although I didn't. I was born and raised in Westchester County, near New York City, and in the minds of people whose families have lived in the town for generations, I would never be considered anything but an outsider.

The sea, in the form of Cape Cod Bay and the Atlantic Ocean, defines the town on the west and east. At its widest point, the land runs five miles from shore to shore; at its narrowest, the ocean wants half a mile to make an island.

North and south, Wellfleet is eight miles long. Tall sand dunes edge the back shore. From the top of them is apparent the arc of the horizon. The ocean before them is by turns ultramarine, cerulean, cobalt, slate, or all of these at once, depending on the light, the depth, the tide, and the activity of the water.

The water is an absorbing presence. People drive up to look at it. They walk along it. They throw stones at it. They shout at it. They reveal themselves to it. It is a tonic and a salve. The water is always cold, even in August. One of the most exquisite satisfactions I know is to run chilled from the water and sprawl face-down in the hot sand.

The bay is usually calm. In January and February it sometimes carries ice the size of small boats. Occasionally the ice piles up and you can walk around out in the harbor channel.

The landscape is spare and uncomplicated and attractive to painters—shades of green and brown pressed in by the sky and the water: the wide blue vistas, the moors, the marshes, the inlets, the bald smelly flats exposed at the lowest tides. The air is free from contamination by anything but salt.

In from the water are ponds and stretches of woods protected by the Cape Cod National Seashore. The ponds are glacial. The woods are recent. An earlier generation deforested the place for lumber. In any of the local historical societies you can always find a picture of your favorite wooded hill as bald as an egg. In the winter you can see long distances through the woods, and you can hear for miles. Standing on the shore of a pond you can hear the ocean. On the beach you can sometimes hear the church bells ringing ship's time in town.

The woods themselves are mostly pine and oak. The pine trees shift and make noises in the wind. It has always spooked me to walk through the woods at night and hear the trees creak.

In the center of town, on Main Street, in a row of plain buildings, there is a grocery, a pharmacy, a variety store that sells newspapers, a thrift shop, a restaurant, a boardinghouse, a liquor store, a funeral home, a church, a town hall (which also houses the library), a bank, and a post office. During the year I worked as a policeman there were a few seasonal businesses—a photographic gallery that also developed and printed film, another restaurant, a store that sold leather goods, a penny-candy store, an art gallery, and two clothes stores. The candy store, the leather shop, and the art gallery abutted each other. The following summer they burned to the ground and were not rebuilt. The lot where they stood is overgrown.

As in any small town, a few buildings need attention. A fence is broken here, a gutter loose there, several houses want paint. A car hit the front of one a few years back, and the owner's idea of repair was to cover the damage with sheets of plywood, which he left unpainted. Some are empty and a few are eyesores.

Around the harbor and on the hills above it are a number of old houses, with dormers, gables, mansard roofs, lacy ornamental work, and additions here and there in response to no particular design except necessity. No one house matches another, and all are overdressed. They sit like a group of old women with their best hats on.

Roughly two thousand people live in Wellfleet in the winter, many of them scratching out whatever kind of living they can: some are carpenters; a few bus dishes, wait tables, or cook at one of the restaurants that stay open; some clerk at the supermarket; a few are artists; some fish the bay and the ocean; some teach school; a few are lawyers, specializing in real estate, speeding tickets, and divorce; some work several jobs at once; and a small, footloose number manage enough weeks of summer work to qualify for unemployment money over the winter. The poverty of the winter is serious.

Until I worked as a policeman I had never spent a fall, winter, or spring on the Cape. I had only been there summers, which meant that over the years I had played tennis, gone sailing and fishing, danced at the yacht club, dug clams, taken swimming lessons, walks, and picnics, and spent days at the beach with other children and adults I was likely to see on one occasion or another over the winter in New York. Whenever I turned up in Wellfleet for Thanksgiving, Christmas, or Easter, as my family often did, I never recognized a face I saw. As a child I heard my father talk about the natives, which brought to my mind something very specific, and for years it escaped me why I never saw on Main Street any dark, smooth-skinned people wearing headdresses and carrying spears.

The oldest local people—that is, the people from the oldest families—are Yankees, with terse purposeful names like Crowell, Atwood, Snow, Dyer, Baker, Newcomb, and Adams, and as a rule they are aloof and all but invisible to the summer people. In general they are exceptionally proud, and I don't know that many of them would like to mix. I know now that some of the local people are taciturn, secret-keeping, blasphemous, eccentric, doubtful, mistrusting, cunning, cranky, thoughtless, peevish, petty, and gossipy. Some have mean streaks a mile wide and they indulge them whenever it appeals. Others I know are generous, patient, hard-working, guileless, reliable, and decent.

Wellfleet's police department was established in 1947 by a vote of forty-two to twelve at the annual town meeting. For a time there was only a chief, and there were call boxes situated around the town. If he happened to be near one when you called, then you could do business. If he wasn't, and you couldn't get hold of him at home, you had to contact the state police, who at that time had a barracks in Eastham, the town to the south. In 1952 Wellfleet bought a radio, and signals were dispatched from an apartment over the fire station on Commercial Street. A family was engaged to live there and answer the phone and work the radio. As the town grew, so did the number of calls, and when a family willing to be frequently disturbed at all hours could no longer be found, the town began hiring dispatchers. And the department grew from one man to two, then three, then four, and so on. I made it a nine-man department.

I saw an ad on the Town Hall bulletin board and went to the police station with my resume. I was sure I hadn't a chance of being hired. To begin with, I am not tall and I am lightly built. (A training manual I read later told me I could create an illusion of height in the public's eye by wearing my hat at all times; its peaked crown was designed for that effect.) Also, I was not a local person and I thought that would make a difference. In addition to all that, several years earlier my parents, having had enough of New York City, had moved to their Cape house. Because of an interest in conservation my father had got involved in local politics. He was appointed by the selectmen to the Conservation Commission, was elected chairman, and afterward found himself in conflict with the selectmen on several occasions. He is outspoken and impatient and sees no reason not to call a spade a spade, and in the end he was bounced off the commission. I didn't think the selectmen would hand his son a town job, but I was curious to see how far I would get.

The Wellfleet police station was then and is still in the small apartment above the fire station on Commercial Street. There is a long, broken-down outdoor staircase leading up to the door. When I arrived, one cop was addressing the dispatcher and another cop. I could see that he was aware of me, but he did not break off his story.

"The guy had this gigantic house," he was saying. "He was probably, oh, I guess, seventy-five, seventy-six, around there. And gross? Easily two hundred and fifty pounds. And not that tall. Stubby type of a guy. So, anyway, he was going to die, he had a bad heart, he knew it, doctor had told him. So what he does is, just before he dies, he decides to go upstairs, and he found the smallest room he could find, it was a closet, practically, just a cot, a bureau, and a window, and he sits down, takes off his shoes, opens the window, says his prayers, crosses himself, and keels over. That was it. Gone. Split. Dead. Then we get the call. Maid found him or somebody. Go get him. Well, let me tell you, it took us an hour and fifteen minutes to move him out of there. *We* pushed, *we* pulled, *we* tugged, *we* lifted. And there's three of us in there, mind you, plus the guy makes four, so you could barely stand, let alone move. And right across the hall was a big master bedroom. He *could* have gone in there."

Then he turned to me. "What can I do for you?"

I said I wanted to apply for the policeman's job and handed him my resume. He took it, shook my hand, laughed, and said, "I'll see that the chief gets it." I learned later why he had laughed: no one ever hands in a resume; they fill out an application.

On one of the days following I had an interview with the three selectmen and the chief. The chief was a large-boned man, with a square head and jaw, blond hair, and puffy cheeks. He weighed close to two hundred pounds. He was wearing dark glasses, cowboy boots, and a Sam Browne belt. One of the selectmen introduced us. "This is Alec Wilkinson," he said. "He has a degree in music."

The chief said, "Music, huh? *That'*ll be a big help. You ought to fit right in on the department."

A year later, when I had got to know him a bit, and liked him, I asked why he had hired me.

"Well," he said, "it happened like this: there was another fellow, and he was more similar to my way of thinking, but he was committed to a job somewhere else. That left you and another fellow, and he was unacceptable."

Because I felt that I should, I told the chief and the selectmen at the interview that I meant to stay only one year at the job. For all I know, this was a relief to them.

It costs the town, or it did in those days, roughly twenty-five hundred dollars in expenses and tuition to train a new policeman. The police academy is in Barnstable, thirty-five miles to the south, and the recruit is legally required to attend the first session held after his hiring. The annual twelve-week course begins in January, and I should have gone, but since I wasn't going to be permanent, the chief and the selectmen decided to sidestep the requirement, save their money, and have me trained on the job.

I went to work at eight o'clock on a Saturday evening at the end of May. Gary Joseph, the sergeant, and Paul Francis, one of the patrolmen, were waiting for me. They were both young men.

Gary was short and overweight. He had shiny black hair cut in precise half-circles above his ears and in a straight line across the back of his neck. His face was small and round, with dark eyes and full lips. There were fresh creases down his shirt-sleeves and the legs of his trousers, his badge gleamed, the leather of his holster was new, and his shoes were polished to a reflecting shine. He had a deep voice which he could make even deeper when he wanted to, and he had a tendency to stare. He wasn't unfriendly, but he obviously hadn't made up his mind about me and I found him intimidating.

Paul was short, and also had dark hair. He had a small waist and large shoulders. He wore black combat boots that were scuffed at the toe. He was thin-lipped and serious, but he smiled easily, and I knew before we had anything to say to each other that I was going to like him.

We went into the chief's office and Gary looked around for a gun to give me. He tried a closet and filing cabinet, and then he found a pair in the bottom drawer of the chief's desk. He looked them both over and chose the one in his right hand, and handed it across the desk to me. It was a .38, but I didn't know it at the time. Weeks went by before I thought to ask what kind of gun I had. I did after noticing that everyone else's were bigger than mine and that, unlike theirs, mine didn't shoot flames when I used it.

"Ever shot one of these before?" Gary asked.

"No."

"I'll take you out to the practice range some time and show you what to do with it," Paul said, but he never did.

"Where's the safety?" I asked.

"No safety," the sergeant said.

"You mean it could just go off?"

"No," he said. "It can't just go off by itself. I mean, if you *drop* it I suppose it could go off."

"I won't drop it."

"Good. That's a start."

The sergeant found a gun belt for me, and a holster and some bullets. The holster fit but the belt was too large, and when I stood up it slid to the floor. The sergeant groaned. I couldn't use the belt until I could make a smaller hole. I was sorry to give it up because it looked professional—it was black leather and had a pattern stitched into it—and I liked it. I strapped the holster onto my trouser belt, which barely held it. The holster had a strap over the top that fit over the hammer of the gun and kept it from falling out.

The sergeant said, "All right, you're all set." Then he turned to Paul. "Take him out and show him how to make some traffic stops." And again to me. "Do whatever he tells you. That way you won't get hurt."

Paul and I went downstairs and drove off in one of the town's two police cars. I was very excited. We stopped at an intersection. A car passed us and Paul turned his head to follow it.

"I'm always observing a vehicle going by," he said. "You keep a mental notebook—the license plate, the color, the year, the condition, the type, the driver, the passengers, where it's going, or where it's just come from, anyone along the side of the road. You never know when you'll use it. Down in Provincetown they got murders. By Jesus, the guys that did it drove through this town surer than shit. They *could* have done it right here and *taken* them to P-town for all we know. So murder could have happened here—and we don't know about it."

The next few hours went by quickly. For some reason, maybe because it happened to be the night of a full moon, everybody seemed jumpy and there was plenty to do. We hadn't even had a chance to stop a car before the dispatcher said, "Charlie One, B and E in progress, Streaves house, Ocean View Drive." Charlie One was the name of the cruiser we were in.

"What's B and E?" I said.

"Breaking and entering. Nighttime like this, it's a felony."

The Streaves house, which I knew because it was not far from my parents' house, had an alarm system that was connected to the police station by means of the telephone wires. It was a summer house and should have been empty.

The way to the house was down a two-lane back road. Paul used both sides of it, drifting into the corners and coming out of them wide, all wheels off the ground at times and on again with a wallop. The engine whined, the tires squealed. I held on with both hands to the barrel of a shotgun, which was set in the vertical bracket in front of me. Paul managed to get one hand on the radio mike and called the dispatcher. "That alarm still on?" he asked.

"Affirmative."

We turned down a one-lane sand road and went about a quarter of a mile through the woods until we came to the house, by itself on a bluff overlooking the ocean. The house was dark, there was a car parked in front of it, the alarm was still ringing, and the front door was open. Paul got a flashlight and started forward and I got one and followed. We went ahead practically in step, Paul a little bit in front. When we reached the door he drew his gun, took a breath, turned on his flashlight, and went through the door. He pulled up short. A man standing in shadows a few feet ahead faced him straight on. The man held a flashlight with one hand and trained a gun on him with the other. It was Paul's reflection in a full-length mirror at the end of the hall.

"Jesus Christ," he said.

We crept ahead a few steps. "Get your flashlight," he whispered. "Take the bathroom and the closet there." Paul went straight ahead for the kitchen and I went left, down a hall, inching ahead with a deep sense of caution. I tried to listen for sounds, a floorboard creaking, something, but the alarm covered everything.

There were towels in the closet and the bathroom was empty, but the shower curtain was drawn. I counted to three and jerked the curtain with such force that I nearly tore it loose from its fixture.

Paul opened a door leading upstairs. I saw his light disappear and moved quickly to catch up to it. The stairs led to a living room that faced the ocean and was flooded through picture windows with moonlight. There was a table with some chairs, and a sofa turned toward the view. The moonlight across the water was spectacular. Paul went down a hallway and tried a door. The room was empty. A second room was also empty. He shined his light into a third. I looked over his shoulder. The light played across a man's figure, face down, spread across a bed. Paul turned the light on in the room and the man woke up. It was Mr. Streaves. He had come down for the weekend and had forgotten to turn off the alarm. The wind had blown the door open and set it off, and he had slept through all the noise.

We went back to the cruiser. By this time the sergeant had arrived to back us up. He asked what had happened. "False alarm," Paul said. He told the dispatcher that we were finished with the call, and she said she had another B & E. She gave him an address in the center of town. Paul took us back to town at speed. Waiting for us in the driveway of a ranch-style house was a woman, about forty-five, in Bermuda shorts and a sleeveless blouse, and a short, heavy man with a crewcut. The woman looked really angry. Paul stopped the car, told the dispatcher that we'd arrived, and as we walked to meet them, the sergeant showed up.

"What's the problem?" Paul said.

"Officer, my son has just arrived for the weekend," she said, "and he and his collection of friends have broken into his grandmother's house, right over there"—she pointed to a house across the street. "Now they *think* they're going to stay there for the weekend. I don't know where they got the idea, but I have news for them. Officer, I want you to find him, he has a red Chevy convertible, an old one, with a big dent in the door that was never there when his stepfather and I drove it, I can promise you that. It has a black top. His name is David Calish and he must be around town somewhere, because they left all their things behind. When I get my hands on him I'll wring his neck. My mother's in Florida and she's just going to be sick when I tell her about this. I want you to find him, and when you do I want him arrested. He can't do this."

The sergeant said, "This is a serious charge, ma'am, and once we get started on it we have to take it to court."

"I don't care," she said. "He needs to learn his lesson, and it might as well be now. I want him arrested, and then we'll see if he ever tries anything like this again."

We searched the house. The kids had broken a window in the basement to get in, but there was no other damage.

The sergeant went back to see the woman. "There's no one here now," he said, "but if they return, give us a call. We'll keep an eye on the place from time to time."

As we walked back to the cruisers he said, "Jeez, what a nut."

Paul and I drove out to Chequesset Neck by way of the road along the bay. The land was a deep, deep blue. We came over the top of a hill and I could see the buoys marking the channel and the flashing red light at the end of the jetty, and the boats at anchor inside it. In the light from the moon, I could find the sticks setting off the shellfish beds in the harbor. Paul said, "What I like about this job is snooping around, being on the prowl," and I realized that was what I was enjoying, too.

We stopped at the yacht club. There were cars in the parking lot, but no lights on in the building. A man was standing by the door with a beer in his hand. Paul got out and approached him, and I followed. "Hey, Pauly," the man said. And Paul said, "How're you doing, Carl."

There was a stag party going on inside for the brother of the man who was standing at the door. On a screen in front of twenty or so men, some of whose faces I recognized but didn't have names for, a man was undressing a dark, Latin woman. He had the full support of the audience. They were steamed up and cheering and shouting encouragement and advice, and they all moaned together a moment later when the projector broke and melted the film. Paul and I left as the lights came on.

When we reached the cruiser, the dispatcher was calling. "Charlie One," she said, "complainant called, subjects have returned to that residence." We went to the house in the center of town again. The sergeant arrived at the same time we did.

A kid was coming out the front door, and when he saw us he ran back into the house. The sergeant led us onto the porch and in the door. The kids were collecting sleeping bags and coats and shoes. The sergeant said to me, "Go and watch the back of the house. You find anyone, bring them back here."

I took up a position on the lawn. In a moment a window opened and a kid climbed out. I shone my light on him and said, "Come over here."

"Are we in trouble?" he asked.

"I really don't know. This is my first night."

I walked him over to the porch. Gary and Paul were writing down names and addresses on a clipboard. The mother and son were arguing on another corner of the porch. Two boys walked over to talk to the one with me.

"He's all right," my prisoner said, pointing to me.

"We were going to clean the place up," one of them said, "and we were going to fix the window in the morning when the hardware store opened. David's grandmother owns the house and she said he could stay there any time he wants."

"I guess the mother's just a little upset," I said.

"She's always upset," he said. "It's her normal condition."

The mother decided not to press charges. The kids got in their cars to leave. They'd come from a town near Boston. We had to help jump-start one of their cars before they could go. "One of them bastards called me a rent-a-cop," Paul said as they left.

Paul took me to check on The Pub. The Pub occupied the bottom floor of a squat two-story building down near the wharf. There were rooms above the bar, and years ago, under a different name and management, it had not exactly been a bordello, but the owner, now dead, could arrange something for you if he had notice. There was a parking lot on the west side of the building that faced directly onto the beach and gave an uninterrupted view of the harbor. During days of too much wind, or bad weather, or when the tide was not right for them to work, or their boats were being repaired, some of the fishermen sat it out in The Pub. At night, during the summer, The Pub usually had a band, and it did a good business, mostly on beer, which the owner complained about; he said he would never get rich selling beer.

As it happened, my first night as a policeman was the night of a total lunar eclipse and when we arrived at The Pub, there was a crowd of people in the parking lot who had come out of the bar to watch it. Paul nosed the car into the lot and then stopped because he couldn't go any farther. We were boxed in by the crowd and two cars in front of us, which weren't moving either. There were kids everywhere. They were all yelling and jumping and whistling and shaking up beers and spraying them around. More and more people arrived and more came out of the bar to watch, and the crowd grew and filled the space around us. I began to feel hemmed-in, and as if I were on display. The moon was nearly covered. As it disappeared, someone in the crowd shouted, "Who stole the moon?" A few voices here and there picked it up. "Who stole the moon?" "Who stole the moon?" In a few more seconds it took totally. "WHO STOLE the MOON? ... WHO STOLE the MOON?" People began clapping the rhythm; someone struck two garbage-can lids as cymbals. "WHO STOLE the MOON? ... WHO STOLE the MOON? ... WHO STOLE the MOON?" Someone else added a grunt on each fourth beat, and this became popular. "WHO STOLE the MOON? *huh* WHO STOLE the MOON? *huh*." It went on and on and on and then finally the two cars in front of us moved and (WHO STOLE the MOON? *huh* WHO STOLE the MOON? *huh*) the crowd opened up. As we drove off, the chant climaxed in a great cheer.

Having sensed at least a part of my thoughts, Paul said, "The first six months were murder for me. After that, when I found out the people I *thought* were my friends weren't really my friends, I felt better off."

At midnight, when his shift was over, Paul took me back to the station. There I met Billy Brooks, who was working the midnight-to-eight shift as a disciplinary measure because he had recently been in an accident with one of the cruisers. It was his birthday; he was twenty-four years old.

"I guess that means twenty-four arrests tonight," he said, as he and I got into the cruiser. After a couple of hours we parked at a gas station, which was closed, on Route 6, the highway through town, and Billy turned the lights off. "Let's see if we can't catch ourselves a live one," he said. It was after two-thirty, and it had been some time since we had seen a car, so I wasn't really sure what he meant. I figured he meant a speeder. He settled himself down in the seat.

"What's it like to work midnight-to-eights?" I asked.

"It's not so bad as you'd think," he said. "I have it down to where I only need about five hours' sleep a day."

Within two minutes he was snoring.

2.

EIGHT AT NIGHT until four in the morning became my regular working shift, and during July and August I spent half of it riding around in the car and the other half patrolling Main Street on foot. I worked Main Street in two shifts, four hours a night, from eight until ten and from midnight until two; I walked several miles a night, I stood around a lot, and my feet hurt all summer.

In the past, the job of covering Main Street during the tourist season had fallen mostly to the specials, the local men who are hired to work part-time in the summer in order to augment the force, but that summer the chief made an exception because he felt I was in need of experience and would get some on Main Street. In fact, what he had said was, "You'll get knocked down a few times up there, I guess. One guy I remember, a special, had a *terrible* time. He worked there for several years. He was just about your size, maybe a little bigger, I guess a little bigger. Anyway, the kids walked all over him. Every time he came down on them, told them to move on or something, you know, they threw him in the bushes. *They* told us this; the guy never did. To this very day I can't figure out why he kept coming back. I guess he just liked to walk up and down that street with the uniform on."

I had my troubles, but they came later. At first it was not unpleasant and I was relieved. The two shifts were very different. From eight to ten the street was full of people, mostly families, and of these, sometimes several generations at once. They went in and out of the Lighthouse Restaurant, and the leather store, and the candy shop, and the news store. Kids—I say kids because I don't know a better word to describe the group between, say, ages fifteen and twenty—sat on the Town Hall benches, or gathered on the lawn and figured out what to do with the rest of the evening, or sometimes pooled their money and, if they were all under-age, looked around for someone to buy them something at the liquor store. And there were always people in and out of Aesop's Tables, an expensive summer restaurant across the street from the Lighthouse. As the night went on and the crowds thinned and there was less traffic, I could hear the clinking glasses and the conversation and the laughter from the people on the porch at Aesop's, and I was a little jealous of them for enjoying themselves so much while I was working.

When Paul or someone else dropped me off again at midnight, the street was empty and it had a different kind of life to it. The gaudy inflatable rafts which stood all day in front of the news store had been taken inside, and the lights in the store turned off; sometimes trucks made night deliveries to Lerna's Grocery; on certain nights a man came and cleaned the floors at the Lighthouse, piling the chairs and the tables in the kitchen and singing jazz songs and show tunes to himself while he worked—I would hear them as I walked by; the tenant who lived above the liquor store would come home, unlock the store, and enter through it, which made me think he was probably the owner; Eddie, the bartender at Aesop's, a man in his early thirties, who spent the winter in California writing screenplays and trying to sell them, would close up for the night, turn off the lights, and walk toward his house on West Main Street; Boston Charlie, whom I didn't know but I liked because he was always friendly to me and most other people were not, would arrive home after a night of playing washtub bass with the Provincetown Jug Band; Cliff, the man who owned Aesop's, would take his dog for a circuit of the parking lot; two big fat-headed toms would gather in Mrs. Brooks's—that is to say, Billy's mother's—backyard and fight; and the two teenage girls from the Ivy Lodge, the boardinghouse on the corner, who stayed up all night would come out. One of the girls was named Sally; I never knew the other one's name. Sally was dark-haired and schoolgirl pretty. She was fifteen and she was also pregnant. She once showed me a marriage license, issued in Texas, that had her name on it, but I never saw or heard of her husband. She used to carry the license around in her pocket. Sally's friend drove a rust-colored Rambler, and each night she and Sally got in the car, took

it around the block, sat in it and talked and smoked cigarettes for a while, and then drove it around the block again.

I felt a part of this scene and that I would be missed
if I weren't there. The Lighthouse man, the liquor-store
tenant, Eddie, Cliff, Boston Charlie, the deliverymen at
Lerna's, the Ivy Lodge girls, especially the Ivy Lodge girls,
might all wonder, if I were missing, where I was, as I did
when any of them failed to appear on time.

I would rather have been riding around in the car,
though. As I walked, I would hear the dispatcher give
out calls on the portable radio I carried—calls for a fire,
or an accident, or a chase, or a medical rescue—and I
would hear, too, the quick, tense conversations back and
forth between the cruisers as they were on their way
there or after they arrived, requesting an ambulance or a
backup of cruisers from Truro, and I began to have the
feeling that everything exciting happened while I was
stuck on Main Street. It wasn't true, but it didn't make
staying there any easier.

The police department had a key to the Lighthouse,
which had been given to them by the owner, and we used
it after hours. I spent a part of every Main Street tour
there, always after midnight when there was nothing else
to do but referee cat fights. Because it was the only place
I could sit without being seen and at the same time be
protected from the mosquitoes, it became a refuge for me,
where I read—I kept books behind a loose board in the
bathroom—or wrote letters on the back of placemats that
had a map of Cape Cod and "Places of Interest" on the
side that was supposed to be up. I enjoyed the stillness

of the restaurant, which at that time of night was like an empty theater set. Before leaving, I drew a glass of water and washed down the caffeine pills I consumed like vitamins that summer in order to stay awake until four.

Some of the others had borrowed the department's key to the Lighthouse and had had it copied. I hadn't, so unless I found a door or a window open—and each night I tried them all, hardly ever with success—I had to wait for the sergeant or one of the patrolmen to come by and let me in. When the sergeant went in too, I usually stayed for a moment and then excused myself, saying I wasn't hungry. I was uncomfortable anywhere with him; I never knew what to say. While he was in the kitchen I would slip over and unlock the side door, and when he left I would go back in.

Usually, from midnight on, when I wasn't in the Lighthouse reading, I was outside reading. Reading on duty—that is, reading anything that didn't have directly to do with the job—was strictly against department rules, but I didn't learn that for a while (although I should have figured out), and I never made any attempt to conceal mine. I sat on the benches in front of Town Hall, empty now, and read with my flashlight. The sergeant would drive past sometimes and just stare. I was so blatant about it that I don't think he knew how to approach the problem. Finally he spoke to me. "You can't read while you're on Main Street," he said. "It looks bad to see a cop sitting down."

One night Sally came out of the Ivy Lodge with a guitar. She knew some chords, but she couldn't tune it. I offered to, and she handed it to me. It wasn't in my hands long before the sergeant drove up. He looked at Sally, then at the guitar, then at me, then at the shape of Sally's stomach, and then he drove away. He never mentioned it.

A LITTLE AFTER eight on a warm evening around the end of my fourth week on Main Street I made my first arrest. I did not pull it off in the most professional manner—in fact, in a letter to someone I know, Joe Hogan, one of the other officers, wrote, "To say that it didn't go well for his first attempt at upholding the law is an understatement." But I got the job done. I got the man off the street.

The generation of kids who tossed my predecessor into the bushes had been replaced by one much less active. The kids I knew liked to group around the benches on the Town Hall lawn and drink beer, or wine, or—and only every once in a while—cheap whiskey from bottles wrapped in paper bags, and watch the traffic. They rarely had too much—there were usually too many of them and the bottle too small—but occasionally someone would get drunk and begin shouting raw remarks, and then one of his friends would drag him off somewhere and sober him up. The town had a by-law against drinking in public, and under instructions from the selectmen and the sergeant I made a stab at enforcing it. Paul told me I should take the liquor away from them and pour it out on the street and move them on. He was probably right, but I had a feeling that had ticket to the bushes written all over it. Instead I asked them to drink somewhere else, and let them know that I didn't care where, as long as I didn't see them.

I arrived on Main Street by walking up Bank Street from the police station. Each night it seemed I had the same crowd of kids in front of me, and after a while I was warning them as many as three or four times a night. There were no confrontations, but they weren't moving, either. The sergeant said he was getting heat from the selectmen to have the place cleared, but they only moved when he showed up.

When I arrived this particular evening, there was a gathering around a car in the parking lot. There were a few beers and a bottle of wine. I made my usual speech: "Drinking in public not allowed . . . could be arrested for it . . . somewhere else."

"Oh, we didn't know that, Officer. I didn't know that, Pete. Did you know that?"

I walked to the post office, at the other end of the street. I had made up my mind that I was going to arrest anyone drinking when I returned. I took from my pocket the piece of paper on which I had written the town ordinance about drinking in public, and checked it because I had the idea that misquoting the statute number allowed a technicality that would overturn the arrest later in court. When I got back, another car had arrived and the crowd was larger by three or four people. As the sergeant had told me to do whenever I needed help, I called the dispatcher and asked her to have a cruiser meet me on Main Street. I was so nervous I forgot to tell her exactly where. Without waiting for the car to arrive—and this was a very sorry mistake—I walked up to the closest person—a wiry, brown-haired kid wearing a t-shirt and blue jeans—and (I was certain I had been told, and I was wrong about this, that in order to make an arrest legal you had to touch the person) placed my hand on his arm. Without knowing it, I had picked someone who had just arrived and had not heard my warning.

"You're under arrest for the violation of town by-law, article seven section nine, drinking in public." He was aghast. "You have the right to remain silent, anything you say will be used against you in a court of law, you have the right to an attorney—" At this moment I looked up and saw that I was in a circle of hostile faces, and it disconcerted me. I couldn't remember the rest of the speech, though I had rehearsed it and even performed it recently for the chief. At his suggestion I had put a card with the warning written on it inside the brim of my hat. As casually as I could, I removed my hat and, holding it in front of me, managed to read the rest of the speech off the cue card.

"Wait a minute," the kid said.

"Too late, you've already been placed under arrest."

"Oh, yeah? Well, what if I hit you?" He raised his fist and held it before me, as if to say, "With this, pal, what if I hit you with this?"

"Then you'll be in more trouble," I said.

"Oh, yeah? Well, what if I run?" And he did—for the woods at the end of the parking lot.

I was so surprised that I just stood there, and then finally I ran too. My gun, my whistle, which had come loose from my shirt pocket and swung at the end of its chain, a flashlight in my pants pocket, a billy club in another, and the radio in yet another all beat against me in different rhythms. At about fifty yards my gun came loose from its holster and fell on the pavement. I heard the sound of it, but didn't realize what it was; I thought someone had thrown a beer can at me. Then I knew, and I turned and saw it lying thirty paces behind me and had to run back and get it. I started off again just as my prisoner disappeared into the woods, and I kept going, even though I knew it was hopeless. The woods were so thick with vines and bushes that he could practically have been underfoot without my knowing it.

The department had a code system for the radio: code one meant "respond when convenient," code two "as soon as possible," and code three, "urgent." I put in a code two and a half, because I knew it wasn't life or death, but I wanted help right away. I didn't really think we could find him, but I just felt it would be better as soon as someone else was there.

Paul arrived first and found me at the edge of the woods, staring into them. I told him I had just arrested someone. He asked me where the arrested person was. I said I didn't know.

"You don't know? What the hell happened?"

"He split. He's in the woods somewhere."

"You know who it was?"

When I said I didn't, he said, "Oh, for Christ's sake," and then, "Come on, let's take a look."

We moved to opposite ends of the parking lot, and then out into the woods, making for each other, looking above into the trees and below into the brush and the windfalls. I couldn't see anything, and standing still and listening I couldn't hear anything either. The one time I thought I did, it was Paul. I was on a small slope, at the bottom of which was a marsh, then a small stagnant pond surrounded by more woods. There were ways around the marsh and the pond, and any number of ways out of the woods. We went back to the cruiser. "I guess we lost him," Paul said. He seemed amused more than angry, and I was grateful for that, but I felt like a total fool. I thought of the man who was always thrown in the bushes.

When we got to the cruiser, Joe Hogan was on the radio. He had stopped a kid walking on the road that bordered the far side of the woods, and he wanted me to come and look at him. We drove over, but it wasn't the right one and we went back to Main Street. I was depressed. We stopped at the crowd of kids, who were still standing by their cars, and I asked them who their friend was. I even threatened to arrest more of them if they didn't tell me. They laughed.

Paul drove the car to the back of the lot and made a slow circuit along the edge of the woods. Suddenly he braked. "What was that?" he said, and was out of the car and into the woods. I hadn't seen anything, but I followed him. There is a garage at the end of the lot, just big enough for one car. Paul went around one side, and I went around the other and ran into a girl—one of the Main Street crowd—crouching next to the wall. I followed the sound of Paul's voice, turned the corner, and saw him standing at the top of a twenty-foot incline looking down on the kid. The girl must have come back when she thought we had left to see if she could find him and tell him that the coast was clear.

"That's my man," I said. It felt so good to see him again. Joe and the sergeant arrived.

"That the guy?" Joe said.

I nodded. Then to him he said, "What the hell are you doing down there, asshole, come up here."

The kid wanted to know who Joe thought he was talking to.

"I'm talking to you. Come up here."

"I'm coming up to knock your head off," he said. He scrambled up, and when he reached the top, Paul, Joe, the sergeant, and I were waiting for him. I say I was waiting for him. Actually Paul, Joe, and the sergeant were waiting for him, and I was standing behind them, waiting to see what he would do.

The kid said, "Gary, what is this? Who is this rookie asshole?" Paul reached out his hand for the kid. I guess he meant to put handcuffs on him. The kid said, "Fuck off, don't touch me."

The sergeant said, "Calm down, Joey." I thought it was peculiar that they should know each other, and that he could talk to the sergeant like that.

The kid turned to me. "I've lived here longer than you, you fucking turkey." Then to Gary, "You can unarrest me, you know, Gary."

The sergeant said he couldn't and asked him again to calm down.

Joe turned to me. "Is this man under arrest?"

"Yes, he is,"

Joe grabbed the kid by the arm to lead him to the open back door of the cruiser. The kid thought Joe was trying to hit him, and he shook loose and swung for Joe's jaw. Joe raised his arms in front of him, as a block, and bounced on the balls of his feet, like a fighter.

"You didn't want to do that," Joe said.

"I did too," the kid said.

According to the way Paul wrote it in his report, this is what happened next: "He then ran, myself right on his tail. I caught up to him; he slipped, and I fell right on top of him. Officer Hogan fell over me."

According to Joe's report: "He was pursued by Officer Francis, Sergeant Joseph, Officer Wilkinson, and myself. He was tackled by Officer Francis and myself."

While they struggled on the pavement to place handcuffs on him, I gathered the flashlights, watches, clubs, glasses, shirt buttons, pens, and change that flew from them in all directions. A crowd had formed, and with my arms full I went up to them and said, "You can all go home now, the fun's over." Actually the fun was in full swing. For a moment, Paul and Joe lost their grip, the kid half stood, and it looked like the chase was about to start over. Paul managed a grip on one arm, and Joe got the other; they pulled him back down and finally got the cuffs on, and then they picked him up. They were all breathing hard and perspiring. Paul's whistle had fallen loose and hung to his waist, the knee of Joe's pants was ripped, and the kid's t-shirt was torn. Joe put him in the back seat and slammed the door. I didn't see how it happened, but apparently the kid lay on his back and began kicking at the window, because it shattered in fragments all over the parking lot as the cruiser sped off for the lock-up in Orleans.

The sergeant said to me, "I want a full report of this on my desk. Tonight. And next time, *wait for the fucking cruiser.*"

He left, and, I learned later, went to inform the kid's parents. His anger, I felt, was justified. The result of my bungling a simple misdemeanor arrest was three felony charges (two counts of assault and battery on a police officer, and one count of malicious destruction for breaking the cruiser window), a considerable amount of trouble for everyone involved, a public display of incompetence (my own, but reflecting on the police department), and the sight of three police officers and a sergeant chasing, tackling, and wrestling into handcuffs—with the expense of much crudely descriptive language—one kid, approximately twenty years old, maybe one hundred and twenty-five pounds, in plain view of summer traffic in the center of town.

At ten o'clock Blocky Burgess, one of the specials, who worked Saturday from ten at night until six in the morning, arrived to spell me. Blocky was probably fifty or so. He had long arms and large hands and the kind of strong, asymmetrically muscled body that many years of physical work make. His regular job was as the highway surveyor, an elected position that meant he looked after the town's roads—saw, among other things, that they were plowed and sanded after snow, and kept free of potholes. As the town goes, it is an important department, with a large budget, and Blocky's position was an executive one. He was gruff and garrulous and I was fond of listening to him. He was also sly and knew the town backwards and forwards. That night Blocky said to me, "Oh, boy, you sure picked a fine one. You'll hear something about this one, for sure."

"About what?"

"There'll be some trouble, wait and see. May happen now, may take a while."

I had no idea what he meant, and I said so.

"Don't you know who that was?"

"Who I arrested?"

"Who else?"

"I never saw him before."

"You'll learn soon enough. I guess goddam so. That was Joey Crowley, the selectman's kid."

Joey's father, Russell, was chairman of the Board of Selectmen, an ex-chief of police, and a popular local politician. Gary had worked as a patrolman under him, which explained how Gary knew the kid, and also Gary's and the kid's agitation. The selectmen had complete control over the hiring and firing of police officers. I wondered if I could lose my job, and Gary must have wondered the same thing about himself. In the end he did go, and so did Joe and Paul, at different times (but within six months of each other), and for different reasons. Yet they were all convinced that their troubles, however long they took to arrive, began that night.

Back at the station I typed up my report and gave it to the sergeant, who had just returned from the Crowleys' house. He took the report from me and said, "What are you charging him with?"

"Drinking in public."

"Where's the evidence?"

Evidence? I couldn't think what he meant. How could there be any evidence if the kid had swallowed it? *"Where's the fucking bottle he was drinking out of?"* I hadn't known I needed the bottle.

At midnight I was back on the street. It was dark and still, and in the parking lot there were only a few little chunks of glass from the window to suggest the havoc of a few hours earlier. Someone, Blocky, I guessed, had swept up the rest. I walked back to the street and stopped by a trash can in front of one of the benches and for no particular reason looked in. A corner of a newspaper from the day before stuck up from underneath a few bottles. The can was full, and I thought it would probably be picked up by one of Blocky's men tomorrow. Then, as if it were coming from very far away, a thought slowly arrived, and I realized that the bottle on top was *the* bottle. I remembered the label and the irregular shape. There was nothing left in it, but I could get it fingerprinted. The sergeant, I felt, would be pleased.

I fastened my fingers on the lip and gently lifted the bottle from the barrel. I walked slowly across the street so as not to even slightly upset it—a less certain grip would have been no grip at all—and made for the station, thinking what a crazy up-and-down night it had been and how I was back on top.

I heard a car approaching from the rear. I never saw who it was, but when the driver was right behind me— maybe I was crossing the street too slowly and he wanted me to get out of the way—he sounded his horn. The bottle slipped from my fingers and seemed almost to float to the ground, where it shattered.

A MONTH LATER, on the eve of the trial, Billy, Paul, Joe, Gary, and I met at the station to rehearse what I would say. They wanted to walk me through it because I had never been in court before. They all agreed I would have had a better case with the bottle. One of them told me that he had heard from an ex-patrolman about a former chief. That chief, the patrolman said, was a heavy drinker, and he would raid the evidence closet from time to time and finish off the bottles. He was not particular, and he would drink whatever they had. When trials came up, the cops had to stop at the liquor store on the way to court, buy another bottle, empty half of it on the ground, and take the rest to court as the evidence.

Billy represented the prosecution and said, "State your name and occupation, please."

Before I could answer, Joe said, "You say, 'Alec Wilkinson, police officer for the town of Wellfleet.'"

"Officer Wilkinson," Billy said, "on the evening of July twenty-sixth, did you happen to see the defendant while in the performance of your duties?"

"You say yes," said Joe.

"Will you explain the circumstances to the court, please."

Three times I repeated the story. Joe interrupted me again and again with "you can't say that" or "leave that out, it's not helpful" or "don't forget to tell them that." I realized he felt I wasn't very smart.

The next morning went pretty much as we had rehearsed it. I told the judge what I had seen, and when I got off the stand and sat down, the sergeant whispered, "You did all right." The defense lawyer was less supportive. He called me a summer complaint—what the locals call an annoying tourist—and said that my appearing without any evidence to support my charge was not only ridiculous, but also a waste of the court's time. He asked that the charge of drinking in public be dropped. Charge dropped. He then proposed that what had come afterward had simply been a justifiable response to an unwarranted arrest. Request to drop second set of charges denied, guilty on all three counts.

Before sentencing, the court called a recess and we went out to lunch. Paul, Joe, and Gary agreed to ask for the maximum sentence. "This job is difficult enough without having someone think they can hit you and get away with it," Joe said. They asked, but the judge suspended the sentence and gave probation.

On a Saturday night a year and a half later, more than seven months since my year as a policeman had expired, I was playing music with some friends in a local bar. My back was to the audience and I was tuning my guitar, and I was jumped from behind. I don't know why, really, except out of a kind of intuition, but I knew it was the selectman's son. I went down and everything stopped and some people pulled him off me and when I stood up, one of the Main Street kids, old enough now to be in a bar, came up to me. He said, "You know what that's for, don't you?" I turned away and someone else came up to me. He was shaking his head and smiling and he said, "Man, you must be sleeping with his wife."

After thinking about it a few days I decided to press charges, but I didn't really want to. I just didn't see any alternative. I didn't feel you let someone jump you in a bar over a grudge, and then say, "We're even." Before I went to the court I met with the chief, the boy's father, and the boy's brother-in-law, who was a local attorney, to see if they could provide me with any reason why I shouldn't go ahead. The father said it would be bad publicity for the police department, and I should consider that, but I couldn't see how that had any bearing. He then said his son had done it because he felt I had lied at his trial and caused his conviction. It was the son's view that Joe had struck him first, and that in swinging at Joe he was only protecting himself.

I filed the charges and dropped them several days later, when I realized that the son was already on probation for the previous assault-and-battery charges brought by Joe and Paul, and that if he was convicted, which he would likely be—the whole bar saw it—then he would have to go to jail. I didn't think that would be helpful. He and I met one afternoon by arrangement and shook hands. I had to appear in court to explain why I wanted the charges dropped. The judge, who felt he recognized the case as common in his experience, believed that the two of us were drunks, and that it was normal for drunks to fight and we shouldn't waste the court's good time with our quarrels if we were only going to sober up the next day and forget all about them. I said that we had been able to work the matter out between ourselves and were therefore able to save the court time, and he said fine, case closed, and don't ever let me see you in here again.

That was the end of it for me, but I have always wished I had never started it. I wish I had waited for the cruiser. At least then the arrest would have been efficient. No one else would have been involved, there would not have been a chance for it to get out of hand, and the worst that could have happened is the kid would have paid a small fine. Most likely he would have been rebuked. The way it happened served no purpose that I could tell and did no one any good, and the bitter feelings it stirred up did not settle for a long time afterward.

3.

The Chief

"I WAS BORN in 1942 in the Chelsea Naval Hospital. We were living in Dorchester, and my father was in the service. Aviation. I have two sisters; one who lives in Truro, married, and one in Connecticut, married. I'm the oldest. I went to Wellfleet High School the last year they held it here, in the old building up above the highway, before it moved to Orleans . . . There were thirteen kids in the class. Went in the Navy, four years, radarman in the combat information center, on an aircraft carrier in the Atlantic. I didn't ever get over to the other side. Got out of the service and came back to Wellfleet, January 1964. I applied to a number of technical schools, and I ended up going to Wentworth College, in Canton, Mass. Stayed there six months and got married and couldn't afford to continue. Then I had several jobs. I painted cars on the line at the GM plant in Framingham. I worked in a glue factory. Bartlett Glue Factory. They ship all over the world. I mixed glue. They have a formula for it and you make it in these big vats. Then I came back to Wellfleet again. My father had opened up the Gulf station and I went to work for him. He had the idea of my growing into the business, you know, taking it over when he retired. One day the police chief came into the station and said how would I like to work for the police department, as a special. I said I didn't know, and he told me to think about it and give him a call. I went to a series of Friday night training sessions in the basement of Town Hall, and then when I started on patrol I worked sixty hours a week. There were three of us, counting the chief. One guy worked the eight to six at night, and I worked the six to four, six days a week. If you called for help only one guy could show up, the guy on duty in Eastham, or Truro, depending on which end of town you were in, and if you had a fight with six or seven guys going at it, you had trouble. Later, when I went to the police academy, I still worked three days a week, thirty hours. You had to because there was no one else around." (The chief is the only officer in the history of the Wellfleet department to graduate first in his class at the academy.) "The pay was fifty-four hundred a year. Total. But it was really forty-eight. The department was just getting a little bigger then, but the town didn't want to pay any more for a budget, so the chief had the idea we would work forty hours a week for the regular pay, and then twenty hours a week for a dollar an hour, to bring the salary up to where you could buy a loaf of bread with it. That went on for almost a year. We got a raise at the next town meeting, but we still didn't get any overtime. The chief tried to keep our hours down to forty a week, but you can't always control it, you don't know what's going to come up.

"I made sergeant in 1967 and then I resigned a few months later. I had complained to the Board of Selectmen about the chief, who had just fired another patrolman a week earlier, got nowhere, and went into a waiting position as a mechanic. I also fished and then I worked with a crew that was making repairs on Route Six. Then the chief resigned and I went back as a special. In 1970 I was full-time again and in '71 I was back as sergeant. In 1973 Russell Crowley, who was the chief then, resigned, and the selectmen asked me if I would like to be considered for the position. Having seen chiefs come and go, I was reluctant to apply, but when the position was offered, I took it. That was the end of patrol work, and I sort of missed it. It could be slow, but you never knew what was going to happen. In the summer the main problems were the kids. They were all over The Pub, and Main Street, down in the center of town, getting drunk, running around, having car accidents, tearing up the beach. I got a call one day back when I was sergeant the first time to go to the beach. Someone had complained about the surfers. There are rules about it now, but back in those days there weren't any. The chief had left town for the day, and he asked me to stand by for him. I was in my civilian clothes and I went down there to Newcomb Hollow and I could see the kids coming in on their boards, and I could see some guy tell the kid something as he went by, so I could see there was a little argument going on there. So I said 'Hey' and whistled and jumped up and down, and he came walking in on the beach, and people now because I had whistled started coming around me. So I waited until the kid got up to me and I said, 'Police officer, you're under arrest.' People scattered, people really scattered, and all the witnesses disappeared. I found the guy who was in the water, though, and I got his name and he'd been down vacationing for two weeks, and I took the kid to Provincetown and locked him up. The kid took the board with him, and they recorded it there as evidence. Surfboard. They asked me what the charge was and I said, 'Operating to endanger with a surfboard.' The booking officer said, 'That's the craziest complaint I ever heard, you guys are getting crazy up there in Wellfleet.' So the next day I went into the clerk's office to file the complaint, and you wait your turn in line, and when I got up to the desk he said, 'What have you got?' I said, 'Operating to endanger with a surfboard.' He said, '*Is* there such a law?' 'There better be,' I said. 'The kid's downstairs, he's been locked up all night, so there better be such a law!' Well, they checked it, and the kid paid a fine, and they gave him back the board.

"The winter was slow. January and February as a patrolman I just couldn't stand. Very boring, very dull. Only one thing happened that really made an impression on me.

"We had two couples come from off the Cape, and they had hit all the antique places and loaded up at every one of them. Stole everything that wasn't nailed down. They came into the center here to the news store, and there was a little old lady there working—this is eight or nine at night. The four of them just walked in there and took everything off the shelf. They took a box of Timex watches, and radios off the counter, and cigarettes, with her standing there yelling, and walked out, and put them in their car and drove away. So she called the station. I jumped in the cruiser and went up over the hill to Main Street and she's pointing, 'They went that way,' and I went off and caught them in front of the Mobil station just as you get to Route Six there. I asked if they'd just come from Wellfleet center, and they said, 'No, we just came from Provincetown.' I had a description, and it was them, but I wanted to make sure, because I was going to throw some pretty heavy charges at them. So I asked them to come back with me, and they said they would. I had no right to search the car until I had a positive ID, and they weren't under arrest, so I couldn't make them get in the cruiser. They'd have to follow me, and that meant they were going to dump the watches and the radios and the cigarettes on the way back. It just happened that the police chief was over getting cigarettes at the store across the way from where I had stopped them, and he had a radio in his car, so I called him and asked him to follow me back to town. I led, and they were behind, and the chief was behind them. When we got to the Holiday House, the chief called and said, 'They threw something out of the window.' I stopped the car in the middle of the road, and I went back and said, 'Don't throw anything out. I got a radio car behind you, don't throw anything else out of this car.'

"We got back to the center, and the old lady comes out and says, 'That's the one with the purple shirt, and that's the one in the dress, and that's the other one, and that's one of them, too.' So there were four of them, and just the chief and me, and he was in civilian clothes. I walked up to the passenger's side first and opened the door and grabbed the guy right out and put him up against the car. He said, 'Be careful,' not like a request, more like a warning, and I put the cuffs on him. I gave him to the chief, and he started to walk him around the car, but the guy's wife opened the door and jumped out and the guy started yelling and trying to kick, and there was a scramble and the feet got mixed up, and the chief went down and hit his head. He's on the ground, and the wife jumped on top of him. I had the other guy out of the car, and I had to shove him back in and shut the door and go help the chief. She was really giving it to him.

"With all the shouting that's been going on, a crowd has gathered and is watching this, they're yelling, 'You fucking pigs.' Things like that. The other pair in the car were docile, but we had to manhandle the wife to get her off the chief, and the guy's still yelling, he's really worked up, he's shouting, 'Bunch of pigs,' and 'No man ever locks me up that I don't kill,' and 'A man should not be incarcerated,' and all this kind of talk. When the chief and I finally got him and his wife in the cruiser and shut the door on them, we went in their car and got all the knick-knacks. I opened the glove compartment, and where the guy was sitting, there's a loaded thirty-two. Right there where he could have got a hand on it. *Holy Jeez*, I thought, *what am I messing with on Cape Cod, you know, this quiet little place here.*"

4.

THE YEAR I worked on the force, there was an extraordinary happening at the pier. That summer Tom Sturtevant was in his third year as watchman. He was twenty-one years old, tall, serious, shy, and slow-speaking, and he worked the four-to-midnight shift. At five o'clock on a sunny afternoon at the beginning of the second week in July, he stopped on his rounds and watched a boat pass the jetty and slowly enter the inner harbor. About forty-five feet long, gray and tan, with a steel hull, she was an uncommonly sturdy boat for the harbor. Tom watched her for a moment, without any particular impression. He saw boats all summer and was past the point of simple surprise or curiosity. He remembered he had work to do and went on.

Speaking of the boat later, the chief said, "I never saw anything like it before. It was an oddball boat. You could tell right away that it wasn't a pleasure craft. It was a working boat, ocean-going in no uncertain terms. These guys were professionals, no doubt about it. They had radar, depth finders, radios, storage tanks, generators, a hundred-and-ten-horsepower diesel—and if *that* didn't work, they had a mast rigged for sailing. I tell you, they had everything. They had *two* of everything, in case something broke. They had boxes of charts, that's right, boxes of charts. *Boxes* of them. Charts of harbors in Central America, South America, and all up and down the East Coast here. Every port i*ma*ginable."

In addition, she was carrying a ton of marijuana.

The crew, all men in their twenties, tied her up to the outside pier, where the fishermen unload their catches. Two of them found Tom and asked where they could tie up for the night. He pointed to a spot inside the pier. Although he was supposed to, he didn't get their names, or the name of the boat. In the three years he worked there, no one had ever told him to do that, he said later, when I asked him what had happened that night.

By the time the crew had moved and belayed the boat, it was six. They made some phone calls, presumably to their shore confederates, had dinner, and went back to the boat to wait for dark. Tom saw them again around nine-thirty.

"Next thing I know," he said, "they moved to another slip, closer to the parking lot. I asked them what they did that for, and one of them said, 'Oh, well, we have to carry some batteries, put them on the boat.' So I didn't pay too much attention."

Around eleven-thirty Tom saw them again. "I never paid much attention until the last time around punching the clock I see all these guys carrying this stuff, bags and bags of it, and loading it into some vans they had, and I'm walking right by them, you know, while they're doing it. I thought they were carrying sleeping bags or something. 'Hello,' I said, 'how're you doing?' They said, 'Oh, we didn't think *you'd* be here now.' They didn't seem nervous, though. They played a good act. I never knew anything was up. But the other guy"—meaning Roy Dean, who had the midnight-to-eight shift—"come on the watch early, and he saw what they were doing. He knew what they were doing, and I didn't know."

Dean is middle-aged and a widower. He lives alone in a trailer near the harbor. He is a kind man, with a round face and thick glasses, and he likes to be right in the middle of things. He came in about eleven-forty and found Tom over at the finger piers, talking to some people who were unloading their boat.

"I went over to get him and walk back to the shack with him, and, *holy Jesus*, when I saw these guys they had side arms on them. Big, big guns. They were beyond thirty-eights."

(Later I asked Tom if he had seen any guns, and he said, "I didn't pay much attention.")

"Anyway, they had these big sacks they were struggling with, and one of the clowns carrying them says they're dirty laundry, but I could hear it rustling in there, and I knew it wasn't hay. And this is the third load they unloaded that night! Well, the only thing I could think of was how to get Tommy out of there. I was afraid they'd push him in the drink when they saw me, you know. And they would have. You don't pack side arms unless you mean business, right?

"So I told Tommy, 'You're stupid. You left the back door open and there's money on the table.' Now, Tommy knew me well enough that I would never call him stupid. See what I mean? He told me afterwards, 'I knew something was wrong when you said that, because you never talk like that.' That's how well the kid knew me." (Tom says that when Roy told him he had left the door open, he replied, "I did not.") "I grabbed him by the arm, and I told him, 'Just keep walking. Don't look back or nothing. *They're unloading marijuana!* Don't you know that?' And he said, 'Oh, are they?' I told him, when we got back to the harbormaster's shack, to go into the back room and lie down on the floor—it was a precaution—and I grabbed the phone and sat down on the floor and called the police."

Myra Hicks, a part-time dispatcher, answered the phone. She was filling in that summer for one of the regular dispatchers, who was on sick leave. Myra has short, tightly curled white hair, and she is small and compact, like a general. She could be skeptical, even quarrelsome, on occasion, and I am fairly sure she saw dispatching as an executive position more than a service one. Roy said to her, "Send a cruiser down here!" and she said, "Oh, what have you got going, a little fight or something?" He said, "*Will you listen to me and get a cruiser down here!*" He could hear a scratching noise on the wire and deduced they had monitored his phone. "You can do that, you know," he said to me—though, given the circumstances, it was not likely that they had.

Myra called Joe Hogan. "I got a call," he told me. "'Go to the pier.' Could be anything, right? So I *eased* to the pier. Next thing I know, there are people running this way, there are people running that way, the watchman's in a complete state of shock. *'They just unloaded a whole goddam boat full of marijuana,'* he said, *'and two vans just left, and, Jesus Christ, they're going up the road!'* I said, 'What're you talking about?' *'Look over there,'* he said. So I take a ride over to the boat, everybody's left by now, and there are great big hundred-pound sacks of marijuana. Marijuana all in the water, all over the pier, all over the goddam parking lot. I said to myself, 'Jesus Christ, this is international stuff, right? They're making a big drug drop up here.' So I get on the radio and I say, *'Block the goddam bridges! Nobody leaves!'*"

While waiting for the cruiser, Roy Dean had lain beside Tom on the floor of the harbormaster's shack. He was worried that, having monitored his call, the crew would be after him before the cruiser arrived.

"I stayed down," he said, "until Hogan came into the yard. He came in quiet, and when I saw it was a safe distance for me, I ran out and said, 'Take this license number and put it over the machine.' But Hogan wanted to know too much and I had to explain it to him. That took up time. Then he wanted to get on the boat. I said, 'You stay the hell away from it. If there's anyone on that boat, you'll get your head blown off.'"

Joe decided to call for help.

Help was scarce. There are only two police cars in Wellfleet, and according to Joe, the other one was "diddling around in the woods somewhere, and he can't get out, or he's stuck or something."

So Joe went back to talk to Roy.

"What color were the vans?" Joe said.

"I don't know," Roy told him.

"How many were there?"

"I don't know."

"Which way—?"

"I don't know."

"Mass, reg—?"

"I don't know."

"All right," Joe said, "they were vans." Roy said he was sure they were vans.

"So I had all the towns alerted to stop every van they see," Joe said. "Nobody saw any vans. Now, that tells you something, right? They're still in town. Or close by. So I go on the boat, *il*legally. Big stacks of marijuana all over the place, and also a gun. So I go, 'These sons of bitches aren't fooling, right? They got guns.'"

While this was going on down at the pier, I was walking Main Street. For some reason, probably because there weren't enough to go around that night, I didn't have a radio. Someone driving by stopped his car and said, "What's going on at the pier? There are cops everywhere," and I said, "Probably nothing." It's not unlikely that the two vans drove right by me, since by several of the possible routes out of town, Main Street is between the pier and the highway.

At two in the morning, Chickie Berrio picked me up and we went to the pier. Meanwhile, Joe had woken

Billy Brooks and they had prepared a search warrant for the boat. Then they rousted someone from the clerk of courts' office for his signature. Chickie dropped me off and Paul, Billy, Joe, and I went to search the boat. Billy was wearing shorts and a t-shirt he had grabbed when Joe woke him. The rest of us were in uniform. The boat was still tied up where the crew had left her. Her name was *The Mischief.*

We climbed down the ladder and dropped onto the deck. The chief and the sergeant, dressed in civilian clothes, remained above on the catwalk, yelling out whenever we were gone inside the cabin any length of time, "Whatta ya got?"

Inside the cabin there was marijuana everywhere, as thick as dust. It was on the table, the floor, the chairs, and the shelves, in the head, in every cabinet and box we opened, among all the charts and papers, and by the wheel where Joe had found the gun. It seemed amazing that the crew had found the harbor at all.

Paul found a brick of blond hash, about a pound of it, wrapped up and stuffed into a cookie tin. Seeing it, I remembered a night in high school, during spring vacation, when a friend and I drove his MG to Brooklyn and I bought an ounce of it from someone a classmate had put me in touch with. I had paid him $145, but that was five years earlier. I have no idea what Paul's chunk was worth. There was also a smaller piece of dark hash that had a gold seal stamped into it. I had bought this kind, too, fairly often. It cost, if I remember, about $120, and was less potent than the blond, which used to make the room spin.

Billy turned up some vials filled with white liquid that looked like Elmer's Glue-All. The bottles had labels that read "Luv-It" in navy on a baby-blue ground. There were no directions. "I bet it's Spanish fly," Billy said.

I didn't find anything except some documents I couldn't read because they were in Spanish. We left the galley for last, since no one wanted to go in there. Dishes hadn't been washed for days and there was a stench of rotting food. Mixed in with the dishes and rancid butter was more marijuana. Joe said, "Alec, go do that kitchen, so we can finish this thing up."

By the end of the search, we had collected, in a pile: scuba gear; some letters and the South American documents; navigation charts; clothes; suitcases; the loaded gun; a wallet; the brick of hash and the smaller chunk; three burlap bags, one clear plastic sack, and one garbagesized bag of marijuana—about two hundred and fifty pounds in all—and eight bottles of "Luv-It."

Billy, Joe, and Paul began carrying things up the ladder to the cruisers. I swept up the marijuana that was left on the floor, and Billy and I took it away.

When everything was loaded into the cruisers and we were ready to drive off, Roy Dean walked up to the sergeant and said, "If you don't leave somebody here I'm going to call the state police."

"What are you going to do that for?"

"They could come back, couldn't they?"

The sergeant left me, with a radio. "If anybody shows up," he said, "give us a call."

I spent the rest of the night in a phone booth, which was the only place I could find relief from the black flies. The booth was nowhere near the slip where the boat was tied up, although it was in the same part of town. At dawn the wind came up and blew the flies away, and I went to see how the boat was doing. I saw the slip where she was supposed to be, but there was no sign of her. As I started to run toward it, I imagined Roy Dean speaking to the sergeant. "What happened to your *man*?" he would be saying. "I'll tell you what happened. He spent the whole goddam night in the phone booth, is all. Four A.M. and he's on the phone. *They took the boat right out under his nose!*"

When I got closer I saw the top of the mast. The tide was out and the boat had only dropped below the sight-line of the dock.

I drew an easy breath and then something caught my eye: a station wagon, a few hundred feet off, creeping along the edge of the pier. The car braked in front of *The Mischief*, then went as far as the harbormaster's shack, where it turned around and started coming back. I was sure it was someone who had to do with the boat and that it would be a real feather in my cap to catch him. I waved to the driver as a signal to stop, and then I remembered the gun on the boat. I shook my head vigorously and turned my back, but when I looked around a moment later he was still coming. I had no idea what to do. I unstrapped my gun and held my hand at the ready. The car was closing. There were two people in the front seat. Man and a woman. Man driving. I told myself to watch their eyes, that would be the giveaway. *No. The hands. Watch the hands.*

The driver stopped next to me. The car's back seat was folded down and the space was filled with boxes.

"What's in the boxes?" I said.

"Doughnuts." He took the cover off one of the boxes. "For the Bookstore," he said. The Bookstore restaurant was close by. He was the delivery boy for the bakery. He'd heard about *The Mischief* on his CB radio, so he'd stopped by to take a look.

Sherman Merrill, another patrolman, relieved me at eight. I went home and slept all day. In the meantime, federal drug agents arrived and introduced themselves to the chief. They took the marijuana and the rest of the things from the boat and began their own secret investigation. Customs agents, alerted by the Coast Guard, also checked in. From that moment on, the case was out of the hands of the Wellfleet police.

"We wanted to have all the agencies come down," the chief said later, "because you could see the scope of this thing. You'd have to send guys all around the world checking on this, and there goes your budget. So I just went out and everything we had, we gave to them."

On an evening a day or two after *The Mischief* had come in, Joe Hogan and a Truro policeman were parked at the town line, watching the traffic.

"Did you hear what we had today?" the Truro cop said. "A kidnapping. Yeah, no joke. First one ever, I think. This guy comes in this morning and says his kid and a friend were walking past this house on Depot Road last night when a couple of guys jumped out of a car parked by the side of the road, handcuffed the kids, and threw them in the back seat of the car. Then the guys went inside, checked out the house, and when they came back out they let the kids go. The kids said the guys had guns and two-way radios in the car. Crazy stuff, huh?"

Sensing a connection to *The Mischief* Joe asked the other Wellfleet cruiser to cover for him while he went to Truro to talk to the father. The man was irate and he yelled at Joe because no one from the Truro force had been to see him. Earlier in the day he had walked up to the house and taken down the license-plate number of a van parked in the driveway.

Using the number, Joe traced the van to a rental agency in Hyannis. He called the police there and asked them to see if it had been returned yet. While he waited he checked the numbers against the ones Roy Dean had given him. Dean's first three numbers matched the new ones. The Barnstable cops called back. The van had been returned. "That's your van," they said. "Marijuana all over the place." Somehow they'd gotten it to Hyannis, forty miles away, despite its having been seen parked in Truro, and despite an alarm alerting all local police departments, as well as the state police.

Once the connection was made with the van, Joe wanted to get inside the house. He got a John Doe warrant, which allowed him and the people in his party to search for bodies. On a table they found newspaper clippings about the capture in Delaware a week earlier of a boat like *The Mischief* and some marijuana.

"So we had the evidence now," Joe said, "and I went back to get a warrant to take the place apart."

With the second warrant they found, in a sleeping loft, a crumpled paper bag full of money. By this time it was well past midnight.

"So we finished up there," Joe said, "and there was one Truro special who they got to watch the place. They called him up and said, 'Get dressed and go down and watch this house. There's a big, big drug raid coming up, millions of dollars involved and guns and kidnappings.' So he goes down there and he has a portable radio. Jesus Christ, he's frantic. 'Who is this?' he says. 'The Mafia? Or what? I'm just a part-time cop. I teach school for a living. I don't need this.' So we calm him down and he goes and hides in the bushes on a hill behind the house and we leave. Now, there's thousands of us counting money up at the Truro police station and, Jesus Christ, doesn't Ralph Lepore, the Truro chief, get in his own car—he's at his house, you know, we haven't seen him yet—and doesn't he go down there himself, to the house, for whatever reason, at four-thirty in the morning. And we're all edgy as hell because we figure the guys are going to come back to the house and want their money.

"So Lepore sneaks down, but I don't know why. He's in his own car. And this special down there only met Lepore once, when he got hired, so he doesn't know his car, and he's sitting in the bushes, and all of a sudden you hear over the goddam radio, *'Ten-four! Ten-four!'* And he says, *'There's a car coming up the driveway!'* Well. Didn't everybody in the goddam world jump into their cruisers—county investigating officer, two Truro cruisers, one Wellfleet cruiser, Billy Brooks is in his own car with the red flashing lights—and didn't we *pa*rade. We didn't let anyone know we were coming, right? Lights going, tires screeching around the corners, nobody else in the streets and we're going *woo! woo! woo!* with the sirens. Jesus Christ.

"Anyway, doesn't Lepore go up into the driveway. And meanwhile this guy's screaming over the radio the entire time. *'He's coming in the driveway! He's coming up the goddam driveway!'* He's beside himself. Well, so Lepore pulls in the driveway, and backs out, and he's on the road again, and he starts down the street. He didn't *quite* get to the corner and he was surrounded, *surrounded,* by law enforcement officials from the lower Cape. He gets out of his car and there are about five spotlights on his face, and one of the cops has his gun out, and somebody else yells, *'Freeze!'* I thought he would have a heart attack. 'If I'd wanted to,' he said, 'I could have been in goddam Si*b*eria by now. I heard you ten minutes ago. *What's* going on here?'

"Then here comes the cop who was hiding up behind the house, and he comes charging down the road. *'You got him! You got him!'* he says. *'There he is! That's him! That's the car!'* Lepore looks at him and says, 'I'm the *chief,* you asshole!' Then he turns to one of the Truro cops and says, 'Get that goddam car out of my way!' and off he went, mad as a bat. That's the truth. So help me God."

There was $19,990 in the bag. The IRS came to pick up the money. When their agents arrived, one of them wanted to know what had happened to the ten dollars that would have made twenty thousand. "What'd you guys do," he said, "take everyone out for coffee and doughnuts?"

"It's funny to joke sometimes," the chief said, "but that kind of thing burns me up." By that time he had had his fill of federal agents and their secret ways. "There wasn't too much trust between me and federal drugs and customs," he said. "I ran into a problem which I'll never do again by having two federal agencies involved. They wouldn't give each other the time of day, and they wouldn't give *me* the right time of day either."

A few days later, a private detective, hired by the lawyer representing the man who had rented the Truro house, arrived. The detective was a former policeman, and he had come to pick up the money. "He and I didn't hit it off too well," the chief said. "He comes into my office and says, 'I want to know what happened with your men down on the boat there.' I said, 'I don't know.' With a case like that, with all those federal agencies around, I'm not about to tell the defense everything that's going on. Then he says, 'I'm going to proceed with unlawful entry suits against your department.' It wasn't five minutes I was talking to him and he comes up with this. I had enough trouble without having him around."

The detective went out in the town asking questions. The sergeant and the chief preceded him and asked people not to talk to him. This went on for several days. Then the hotel owner told him that his room had been rented, and he had to be out by the next day. He went to see the chief again. "Strange thing just happened, chief," he said. "You didn't get me thrown out of my hotel room, did you?" The chief said he didn't.

In the meantime the chief had written a letter to the editor of the Boston *Globe* to clear up a story that had appeared in that paper the day after *The Mischief* had come in. According to their reporter, the Wellfleet cop answering Roy Dean's call roared to the pier with sirens and lights, disrupting a stake-out by federal agents. No one knew where the reporter's information came from, or why, if there were federal agents there, they let the vans escape. (Later the chief told me that federal agents were expecting *The Mischief*—they thought she and the Delaware boat were part of an eight-to-ten-million-dollar smuggling ring they were keeping tabs on—and they did have a stake-out. In Provincetown.) The *Globe* sent back an apology from the editor and the reporter, and the paper printed a retraction. The chief pinned the reporter's letter and the article to his wall, and it remained there all year.

Some time after it was all over, I asked the chief if he thought Joe had done the right thing that night. "Well, Roy gets on the phone, you know, and he says, 'You better get down here right away.' That doesn't tell anybody anything. And when you come right down to finding that gun by the wheel, it may have been to Hogan's advantage to go to the harbormaster's shack first. See what I mean? Those kind of guys, in that position, with that kind of take in a boat, and the organization that's got to be behind it, no way they're going to get caught. It's probably better that Hogan went straight to the shack and that that's the way Roy called it in, instead of saying,

'At pier so and so there's four guys unloading grass into two vans, and as you come down the road they're straight ahead.' If Hogan had showed up at that pier and blocked those vans and jumped out with a shotgun, we would have had a different story."

Later I asked Joe about it. "That case woke me up," he said. "It really did. I said, *'Why Wellfleet? Did they know I was on?'* It makes you feel that you're not quite as safe as you think you are here, with nothing to do at two in the morning except chase dogs."

We were at his house and he got up to put on some coffee.

"I have no doubt," he continued, "that years from now I will be home trying to take a nap, or the dinner's burning and the kids are screaming and the television's on, and the phone will ring and some guy will say, 'We want you up here in Boston tomorrow to testify on what you know about a drug drop that occurred on your piers in 1975.' This will be years later, I'll be an old man, and I will have moved, and I won't remember the town, or the year, or the people involved, anything I did or saw, right? Nothing."

5.

The Sergeant

IT HAD BEEN the Sergeant's ambition to be a professional baseball player. In order to participate in a college summer league that in the past had supplied big-league teams with a player or two, he attended a junior college in New Hampshire. On the eve of his first college game he came down with appendicitis. The next spring he broke his pitching arm. He became a bartender.

"I was working in Eastham at the Sandpiper Restaurant," he once told me. "This was April of '71, and Donny Watson, one of the Wellfleet cops at the time, was in there having dinner with his wife. And I always thought if it wasn't going to be baseball, I might like police work. At the beginning, you know, it was just the uniform and so forth. I asked Donny if there were any positions on the Wellfleet force. He didn't know for sure, but he thought there might be and about a week later I had a job. I was a special but I was working forty hours a week. After three months they made me full-time." He had been there four years when I arrived, and had been sergeant for one.

Out of uniform, Gary was different from the person he was in it. On his own he was friendly, sometimes loud, often amusing, certainly gregarious. On the job he was belligerent and abrasive.

"If Gary would change his attitude," one of the others told me, "he would be a damn fine cop. But he has a bad attitude toward everybody, especially when he's with another cop. Then he's king of the world. That's it and no one can touch him. One time I'd like to be off in the shadows, him knowing that I'm there, but let him handle it all by himself, him talking the way he does, and let his ass get kicked one time. But you can't do that. It would straighten him out, though, and do him a lot of good."

The department consensus was that it was only a matter of time before Gary bullied the wrong person and paid for it, but it never happened while I was there.

GARY WAS SHORT and heavy-set, and neither resembled the athlete he had hoped to be nor behaved like one. He lived in an upstairs apartment only two hundred yards from the station, but he seldom walked the distance. The cruiser often picked him up for work, and if he was in the station when his shift ended he took a ride home.

I admired all the men I worked with. Nothing about any of their lives was easy, they worked terrible hours and were deprived of their families (in Gary's case, his wife, who was a dispatcher for the Provincetown police, worked days and he worked nights, and the only day off they had in common was Sunday), they made no money to speak of, no one outside their small group liked them or felt any sympathy for them, and everyone wished them troubles, but I never heard them complain. They were generous and patient and always extremely kind to me. Again and again I gave them reason to throw up their hands, but they never did. No one had more reason than the sergeant. If I had ever made any worse mistakes than I did, or caused another person to be hurt for my lack of knowing the proper way to handle a particular problem—if I had shot someone (and I must have seemed capable of it in a panic)—Gary, as sergeant and man-in-charge of the night shift, would have been called to account for it. The chief or the selectmen would have said, and they probably did after I had arrested Joey Crowley, "Why didn't you keep your eye on him? How could you let him do that? Where the hell were you? When you're on duty and he is too, you're responsible for him." Gary never made me feel the pressure. Instead, he lent me the book in which he kept his notes from the police academy. The entries, on white paper, were carefully typed and centered within a red legal border. It was obviously an important possession and the impulse with which he had offered it was a handsome one.

The sergeant and I were never friends—our relationship was too stylized to admit the kind of intimacies that give rise to friendship—and I have no idea what he had on his mind, but I sensed that a number of things worried him; that he felt pressured to be a model sergeant and wasn't quite sure how to be one, that he was only twenty-five and didn't want all the responsibility he had (as sergeant he was paid only about ten dollars a week more than he would have been as a patrolman), that he was self-conscious, and that he often wished he were different or knew another way to do things. He was not without an awareness that there are people who don't submit to aggression; he also knew that while he was liked by the people he worked with, some of them had reservations, and he had a number of enemies in the town. One evening while we were driving together he said, "They say it takes five years to become a good cop," and though he was ostensibly giving me advice, I knew from his tone that he was assessing himself. It wasn't until later, and after a number of other things had happened to him, that he ever talked to me about some of his worries. Despite being jokey and loud and gruff, and seeming to be all on the surface, he was reflective and kept more to himself than anyone suspected.

"I'M PROUD TO wear the uniform," he said once. "To be a cop you have got to have an open mind, you got to have common sense. It's a big thing in police work. Every person is different, and in a small town you get to know everybody, and you get to know how to deal with certain ones. You got to use force, if it's necessary. If it's not, then don't use it. You got to remember, too, that a police officer

always has the upper hand. So, if you're out to get somebody, or somebody calls you names or something like that,
you place it in the back of your head, and somewhere
along the line they'll screw up, even for the most littlest
thing. It's not a vendetta, it's just that if the guy's breaking
the law he's breaking the law. You might be able to bend
backwards, or do this or that, but maybe you don't in
that case. It's our way of saying, 'Thank you for calling
me a pig.'"

I don't know that he had it in him to be vindictive. I
never saw any indication of it. A year or so later I saw him
be forgiving, or at least accepting, when it was the admi-
rable thing to do.

More than anything, I sensed he was lonely.

6.

I USED TO love driving the police car. I loved the privilege of it, going anywhere I wanted to, up any driveway, down any private road, past any No Trespassing sign; I loved the nervous feeling of speed; I loved being intimate with the special menace of the interior, with the shotgun, the two-way radio, the spotlight, and the heavy black flashlights; I loved the harsh cranky siren and the blue lights on the roof, which made everything—cars, trees, people—look in the dark as if they were underwater; and I loved the sleek, peaceful quiet of it late at night, when not much was happening and the radio was silent and it was possible to glide through the town and the woods, down the highway and past the harbor, disturbing nothing. I never got tired of it.

I also never really got the hang of it. My first night alone in the cruiser I missed a curve and torpedoed into the woods. Another time I hit a tree in such a way that the right rear door of Charlie One could no longer be opened except by being kicked from the inside. Exploring the woods one afternoon, I scraped a pine tree and it left a deep, pitchy scratch half the length of the car. Deep in the woods on another occasion, I misjudged the clearance under a tree limb and shattered one of the blue lights and knocked the new roof rack irreparably out of line. Not long after that, I was parking at the post office and my mind was somewhere else and I drove head-on into the cement retaining wall at the edge of the lot. One day, driving faster than I should have down a sand road, I hit an exposed root and fractured a ball joint, separating the left front wheel from the rest of the car. On a Sunday afternoon, in the center of town, I sped out of a driveway, for no reason except that I was bored, hit a deep pothole I didn't see, and belly-flopped onto Main Street in front of one of the selectmen, who was driving by. He complained to the chief and I got called on the carpet for it. The only time it wasn't my fault I was driving one of the back roads just after midnight. I was going slowly, because I had the sergeant with me and I was being careful not to wake him, and a deer ran from the woods on my right, slammed into the rear fender, collapsing it, and continued into the woods on the other side of the road. I had been making an effort to improve my driving and I had been accident-free for several weeks, and it depressed me that things went wrong no matter what I did.

If there had been a foot patrol in the winter, I would have gotten it, and the only thing that prevented the chief from creating one for me was that he had two men taking courses at the academy and he needed everyone just to cover shifts.

Wellfleet's cruisers were Chevrolets, I forget what models. They were painted two shades of blue, the body darker than the roof. To save money, the chief accepted whatever colors were available that year, rather than order custom paint jobs the way all the other Cape towns did. Because the cars were bought one at a time, on staggered schedules, there was always a period when they were of different years, and the colors didn't match, one car to the other.

The town symbol, an Indian fishing from a beach and some Pilgrims approaching him in a dory, was pasted to each of the front doors. A new copy was painted for each new car, and the sign-painter's interpretation of his previous work was unreliable. One year the Indian fished with a spinning reel.

Wellfleet, sometimes written on the trunk, was one year spelled WELLLFLEET.

When I began working, there was only one real cruiser. The other had been destroyed several weeks before, when a car plowed into the back of it. Billy Brooks had been at the wheel and Charlie Valli was with him. It was just a little after midnight. They saw some hitch-hikers on the highway and they stopped to question them. Billy pulled the car onto the shoulder. Looking up during the conversation, he saw headlights filling the rear-view mirror.

"The next thing I know is this crash," he said later, "and everything inside the cruiser just went haywire. The seat on Charlie's side flopped back, the cage between the seats broke and I whacked my head on it, and the cruiser just sailed down the road. I think the measurement they took from the skid-marks was ninety-three feet. I looked at Charlie and I said, 'Are you all right?' and he said he was, and I got out and said, 'Oh, Jesus, look at the cruiser.' The back was completely stove in. When the chief hears about it he says, 'Was Brooks driving?' It's lucky I had all those witnesses this time."

A few weeks earlier Billy had been in another accident, and in fact was on midnights because of it. Then he had been hot-footing a prisoner to the lock-up in Provincetown, with the blue lights on, when he was cut off by another car. He braked, spun a circle and a half, and ended up backward in a ditch. The prisoner was so drunk he didn't remember what had happened until someone told him the next day, and Billy might have gotten away with it—except that the chief had been having dinner in Provincetown that night, with his parents, and on the way home he passed Billy, in the ditch with the blue lights still flashing. Because of the accident, Billy was not supposed to drive unless he was alone.

Until the new cruiser arrived, the department rented a black Chevy Monte Carlo. It had air conditioning, bucket seats, and an AM radio, all of which were luxuries. The sergeant usually rode in the Monte Carlo in order to listen to the Red Sox games. When the sergeant didn't have it, Joe Hogan did. Hogan was fascinated by sharks, and that summer he used to like to take the Monte Carlo and slip into the drive-in whenever *Jaws* was playing, which was just about all the time, to watch the last few minutes of it. Joe used to park in the back row and turn the lights off, and when the fish rose out of the water to try for the man on the boat he would go rigid.

Making traffic stops with the Monte Carlo was difficult because it was very slow—Chickie used to say it had a V-six that wouldn't pull the hat off your head—and it had no siren, and only a portable blue light that plugged into the cigarette lighter and had to be held on the roof with one hand while you drove with the other, or the light would blow away. You felt ridiculous doing it. Also, in holding the light, your hand covered about half its area and the part of the beam that escaped barely lit up the hood ornament. Usually you had to call the other cruiser for help.

The chief posted a notice on the bulletin board that said no one was to take the Monte Carlo into the woods, and no one did for a while, and then somebody did, and after that everybody else did too. In a few days its finish was scratched beyond the help of anything but a total paint job. I always wondered what the rental dealer's expression was when the car was brought back to him.

THERE IS NO such thing as a paddy wagon on Cape Cod. On the rare occasions when a policeman has a number of prisoners, as he might on, say, Halloween, he uses a school bus to transport them. Otherwise, the policeman puts them in the back seat of his car for the ride to the lock-up.

The back seat was depressing, and I felt sorry for anyone who had to ride there. The floor was always littered. At any time, one might find chewing gum, candy wrappers and candy, napkins, newspapers, plastic wrap, magazines, paper plates, coffee cups, spoons, sugar packets, soda cans, pizza crusts, cigarette butts, and the heavy black and orange rubber raincoats we used. Paul once found two joints a man had ditched in order not to have them on him when he was frisked at the lock-up. He charged the man with possession but lost the case because he was unable to prove that the seat had been cleaned recently and that the joints hadn't been in the general mess on the floor for some time. There were probably also fleas in the back seat, since we carried dogs to the pound whenever the dogcatcher couldn't be located.

There were door handles in the back seat, but the doors didn't open from the inside. The windows opened only enough to allow a trickle of ventilation. Between the back and front seats there was a steel-mesh divider, called a cage. It was composed of small grids, in a diamond pattern, and because of the disturbing way the pattern divided up the image in front of passengers, it gave them a touch of vertigo to look through it. Sometimes it made drunks sick, and then we had to take the back seat completely out of the car and hose it off.

The grids were small enough that hands couldn't slip through them, but smaller things could. I never handcuffed people because they issued me cuffs that Chickie had turned in for a new pair when he lost the key. One night, though, a pair of free hands struck a match and tried to set my hair on fire.

In the front seat on the driver's side of the cab were the grip and switch for the spotlight, which was mounted on the fender. Pointing the light at, say, a blackened section of woods, and turning it on, was like striking a match in a dark and not entirely familiar room. Some nights, by shining its beam into certain stands of trees, or across certain fields, we could catch the light reflected in the eyes of feeding deer. By the same method I found fox cubs in the spring. One night, driving past the cemetery, I switched on the light and it framed an owl. He glared at me, then rose from the branch and flew off beyond the reach of my light. I had never seen an owl before and hadn't been aware of their size, or the reach of their wingspan, or their agility; in making his exit he had dipped among the pines like a swallow.

The police radio sat above the drive-train hump. Its microphone rested in a holder attached to the dashboard. Someone always seemed to be talking on it, but I had no idea what about because they used a code.

The chief had given me a card that had on it an explanation of the radio code and had suggested I keep it with me for the first few weeks so that I could refer to it, but I left it in a shirt pocket, and it went through the wash. I was embarrassed to ask for another, so I tried to pick up the code along the way. Paul would stop a car and say, "Three-seven-zero, zero-thirteen, Mass. X-seven-eight-four-six-five, signal-ten, zero-eight," and I knew that one of those must mean "stopping a car," but which one? And what did the other four mean? I finally asked Joe Hogan for help.

"It's all based on numbers," he said. "Every town has a number for its station, numbers for its cruisers, and numbers for the calls. We're 'three-seven-zero' in Wellfleet. Our cars are Charlie cruisers. P-town's Abel, Truro's Baker." Eastham, the town after Wellfleet, was David, but for some reason Orleans, the town after Eastham, was Mike, and then Chatham after that was Fox, continuing through the alphabet. "We're Charlie One and Two. Now, if you happen to hear that called and you're in the cruiser they're calling, you just pick up the mike and answer, like the telephone. Simple. To call the station you just say the number. Call her and ask for a time check."

"Three-hundred-seventy from—"

"*Three-seven-zero*," Joe said.

The dispatcher answered, I asked for the time, and she gave it to me.

"Not too bad," Joe said. "Now, here's where you get to the codes. *Zero-one* means you're on the air. You say that at the beginning of the shift so the dispatcher knows you're in the car, and she can give you calls.

"*Zero-two* means you're off the air. If you know where you're going to be, give her the phone number. Say 'Zero-two, two-five-four-six,' or whatever.

"*Zero-three* means you're off the air at home, you went home for supper, cup of coffee, something like that. Then she knows she can call you there.

"*Zero-four* means you're off the air at a call. When you get there tell her where it is. 'Zero-four, Pine Point Road,' if it happens to be that.

"*Zero-five* is you're finished with the call and back on the air.

"*Zero-six*, give me a phone call. That's if there's a call you need information about, someone local, maybe, and you don't want to go over the air with it, or it's one with an explanation that would take up too much air time. You give the dispatcher the number of a phone booth, say 'Zero-six,' and the number, and have her call you there.

"If she tells you to *zero-seven* it means to come to the station. Probably there's someone there to see you or some business to take care of. If she says *zero-seven-x*, and you won't hear that too often, then that's an emergency. She's getting attacked or something, and you have to get there right away.

"*Zero-eight*, when you ask for a zero-eight it means you want to know who owns a certain car. You find out by giving her the license-plate number and the state. You got all this?"

"Yeah."

"Okay, you see a car parked somewhere and you want to know who owns it; or you see somebody driving a car, and he looks a little leaky so you want to find out who it is; or you stop a car, and the guy has no registration, and he says it's his sister's car, and you think it might be stolen. Any of these, you might put in a zero-eight. The dispatcher calls the radio shack, which is the clearing house down in Barnstable, and they feed the information into a computer, and it comes back and tells you what kind of car it is, what year, and who owns it, and where they live. Now, if you stopped a Mercedes, and the license plates come back supposed to be on a Pinto, or if the guy's license doesn't match the name of the owner, you know you have something to talk about. You can get a zero-eight for anywhere in the country.

"It can take anywhere from five minutes to five hours to come back, depending on the time of day, and where you want to get the information from. Usually, Alaska's going to take longer than Connecticut. Also, they shut the computer down every night about two or three o'clock for maintenance, and you can't ever get anything then.

"*Zero-nine* just means stand by. You say that to the dispatcher when she's calling you and it means hold the phone, you've got something else going.

"*Zero-ten*, we don't call it that, we say 'signal-ten.' If you ask for that you give the registration, say 'Signal-ten, seven-six-eight-eight-three,' or whatever number it is, and the state, and that goes into the NCIC file, the National Crime Information Center, I think it is, and that tells you if that registration has been reported stolen anywhere. Any time you stop a car and it's full of teenagers and there's beer cans everywhere on the back seat, or it's old, or something don't look right about it, the ignition's popped, whatever, ask for a signal-ten. Usually it comes back right away and then you know where you stand. If it's not stolen, then the dispatcher's going to call you back and say, 'Charlie One, no record Mass. reg. seven-six-eight-eight-three.'

"A *zero-eleven* means on assignment. We don't ever use that one. I don't know why.

"*Zero-twelve* is location. Where you at? The dispatcher will ask you that sometimes to find out which cruiser is closer to a call or, if you want to know where another cruiser is, you might want his help and want to know how long it will take him to arrive, or you want to talk to him, you ask for a zero-twelve.

"*Zero-thirteen* is the one that means you're stopping a car. If you do that, again, give her the license plate and say where you are. If it's not busy with something else, the other cruiser will come give you a backup.

"*Zero-fourteen* means you need help. Emergency, you're getting beat up or something. It's like zero-seven-x for the dispatchers, only this is for you. If you ever hear a cop on the radio say zero-fourteen, then drop everything and go help him.

"So that's it for the codes. There's just a couple of other things. If you stop a guy without a license, you can find out if he's got one by giving the dispatcher his name, birth date, and Social Security number. A computer checks on that. Then there's an M and W, missing and wanted. You use the same information, and it checks out the guy to see if he's escaped from somewhere or maybe got a warrant out. This happens every once in a while.

"Whenever you talk on the radio," Joe said, "you want to do it fast because you don't want to take up air space that somebody else might need for an emergency and because there's people listening on scanners. You don't want to tell them too much."

People with scanners were an irritation. They would hear calls and show up for fires and car accidents and gawk and get in the way. "You get a little crowd of spectators," Billy used to say, "they kick over evidence, little stuff at accidents is evidence. I've seen accidents with gas tanks leaking and gas all over the place and people standing around smoking cigarettes." In addition, a person working with a scanner could break into a house or a store and know the exact moment the police were alerted. Furthermore, the people I worked with, although curious sometimes to the point of rudeness about other people's affairs, were sensitive about their own privacy. Billy used to say, "Your business is our business, and our business is none of your goddam business."

To thwart people with scanners, Paul developed a new code system. He spent a great deal of time on it. He arranged the calls in order of frequency and numbered them, and lettered and numbered the houses and businesses with alarms. After that, calls sounded like "Charlie One, three-three-eight, B-eleven," instead of "Charlie One, you have an alarm at the Holsteins' property."

The new code was a success except occasionally when Freda, one of the senior dispatchers, used both the old and the new. She would send a call, "Charlie One, three-four-two, Ocean View Drive, fourth house on right," and sometimes several minutes later say, "Charlie One, you clear from that domestics yet?"

Underneath the radio were the switches for the loudspeaker, which was capable of stunning blasts. Mounted on the radio box were the controls for the siren; one button operated it manually and another automatically. The siren had two sounds: the *wail*, which was just that, and the *yelp*, a rapid pulsating sound with a sharp, choppy attack. It was a thrill to use either one of them.

Next to the radio on the passenger's side was the shot-gun. There was always one in each cruiser except for the week the chief went hunting in Maine and took one of them with him.

The interior of the cab was done in flat black. In the summer, with the sun on it, the cruiser burned like an oven. It always seemed twenty degrees hotter inside the cruiser than outside, and even the most sweltering days were mild once you got out of the car.

7.

Billy Brooks

BILLY MADE THE arrest in what is, so far as I know, the only bank robbery in Wellfleet's history.

"We got some call at the station, I think it was 'They need some moral support at the bank.' Well, right away when I heard that I sensed a problem. I thought something was strange that they would use that terminology: need some moral support. But nobody at the bank had pushed the panic button—the whole place is wired into the station, you know, and every teller's window has a button.

"So I went up there, I was in ordinary plain clothes, I guess I'd just got back from court, and I stood behind the mirror in the teller's office and watched this guy's transaction, and it looked normal to me. But the guy had used a note that said something like 'Give me the money or the next breath you draw will be through a hole in your head.' I was waiting for the cruiser to arrive before I did anything. The guy was around the bend anyway, I guess. Totally out of it. He'd asked the teller for three hundred dollars, I think it was, because that's how much he needed to pay a repair bill on his car before the garage would give it back. The teller was a woman, and she was scared, but she kept calm. She told him three hundred dollars was a lot of cash to carry around. He agreed and she arranged for him to deposit some of it into a Christmas account for his children, and while she had him tied up with that, my partner arrived. We tackled him and wrestled him to the floor and he's yelling 'Fuck you' this and 'Fuck you' that. I was concerned. With a guy like that you don't know if he's carrying a heater or not. Especially where he's crazy. I carry a gun, he could too. Anyway, he still had the money on him—that is, the part of it he didn't want to deposit."

Billy Brooks is exceptionally tall, large-boned, and slightly heavier than he probably ought to be. He wears glasses, and his face is owlish. He has a mustache and a high forehead, brown curly hair, and eyes that never seem to stop moving. He blushes easily. He looks older than he is, which in those days was twenty-four. He is excitable and inclined to worry and occasionally he has high blood pressure. "I get worked up," he says. "I can't seem to help it. The doctor tells me to relax. I tell him, 'That's easy for you to say.'"

He is formal in his manners, and there is a seriousness about him that suggests he would be reliable if you needed his help. He is intelligent, nervous, ambitious, romantic in the way he sees himself as a policeman, sentimental—he got married on Valentine's Day—and impulsive to the point of recklessness. He is both gregarious and shy. A favorite activity of his when I knew him was to drive the streets of Provincetown during the summer and watch the crowds.

He was married during the year I was there. He kept the ceremony a secret. As far as I know, the only person he told in advance was Peter, the dispatcher, who was his best man. I knew because I happened to drive past the Catholic church in the cruiser as he and his bride were leaving. The girl was a high school senior with whom Billy had had a hot and cold romance for about a year. They lived the rest of that winter in the trailer park by the bay, in a trailer Billy rented that was barely large enough for him to stand up in, along with two Siamese cats, and were divorced in the spring.

Billy was born in Chicago, where his father worked for NBC. The following year Mr. Brooks retired and moved his family to Cape Cod, first to North Truro and then to Wellfleet, where they occupied a large white house with twenty-one rooms on Main Street. Billy's father died when he was young. His mother, who is elderly and under care, no longer lives in the house, though she still owns it, and the place is empty. It is much too large and costly to heat for Billy to live in by himself.

In school Billy excelled in math. "I really liked it, and was heading toward teaching it," he once told me, "but I got into an argument with my high school guidance counselor—I don't even remember what it was about now, but it got bent all out of proportion and very bitter—and it just made me say, 'Forget it, I'm not going to go to college.'" It was a decision he occasionally regretted. He said to me, "Being a cop is not the greatest thing in the world, I guess, but if you're twenty-four and you didn't go to college, what else are you going to do?"

After graduation Billy went to work for the lumber yard in Wellfleet, loading trucks. While he was there the man who was then chief asked him if he would like to join the department as a special. Several months later one of the patrolmen quit and Billy took his job. "When you work part-time," he remarked once, "you see some of the things that go on, the investigations and the court work, and you get to wonder what it would be like to do it full-time."

When I started work, Billy was at the end of a streak of bad luck with the cruiser. He told me about the two most notable occasions, the ones for which he received midnights.

"The guy I was taking to Provincetown had been involved in a hit-and-run, and he was drunk, and I was going about eighty miles an hour down Route Six, and I had the blue lights on, and I came up behind some car, and I was about to pass, and he pulled into the passing lane in front of me, and I swerved, and we went round and round, spinning, and finally backwards into a ditch. I really thought I was on the way out on that one. I had Charlie Valli with me and he was just keying the mike to call ahead to P-town to alert them that we were on our way with a prisoner, and they said later all you could hear over the radio was the squealing of the tires, and then it was just silence. Freda was dispatching that night and I heard afterwards she was crying because she thought we were dead.

"Then there was the time that guy married the back of the cruiser. I had ESP that night. We stopped to talk to a couple of guys hitch-hiking. They were standing out in the middle of the road trying to flag somebody down to pick them up, and I said to one of them, 'You better get off to the side of the road before some drunk comes along,' and for some reason I put the car into neutral and not park. The only thing that saved us, I think, was that the spare hadn't been bolted down and it was entirely inflated and the way the other car hit us, it knocked the spare in as a kind of barrier between the trunk and the back seat. Later they had the guy in the rescue truck on the way to the hospital. I was in the front seat because I had a big goose-egg on my head and my whole head was pounding, and I heard the guy wake up and he said, 'What happened?' and the rescue guy said, 'You don't want to know,' and he said, 'No, really, what happened?' and the other guy told him, 'You hit the police car.' Since then I've been death on drunk drivers."

Although we were roughly the same age, Billy had many more responsibilities and the added pressure of wanting to excel. He was the department prosecutor, which meant that he handled all the misdemeanor court traffic—speeding tickets, drunk-driving arrests and so forth. He was an able prosecutor—in court he was poised and respectful, and he probably won more often than he lost—but he favored plea-bargaining, which no one else did. The others often put some time and imagination into selecting their charges, and it was a matter of pride to follow through on them, especially if they thought they stood a chance of winning a conviction. Paul was especially opposed to reductions of his charges, and whenever Billy would try to convince him of the worth of plea-bargaining in a particular case, he would say, "Jesus Christ, it's the *Let's Make A Deal* show, with your host, Billy Brooks," which wounded Billy. In addition to being prosecutor, Billy was the department narcotics officer. In that position he traveled to various conventions for information and to schools to give programs. He was also involved in investigations. Work piled up on him, and occasionally he had more than he could handle.

"When I walk into the station sometimes my head goes crazy," he said. "I have headaches and my face gets flushed. I haven't been able to determine why. I don't know if it's nerves, or what it is. It's just the pressure, I guess. The stress. You get it from all sides. When you go into court it's the police officer who seems to be on trial, not the defendant; the cop's the one who gets ridiculed, and people try to poke holes in his story. When you're working, the town is always watching. It's unfortunate that everybody in town here knows all the cops by their first names. I'm not sure that's healthy. Being the police you like to have the upper hand, but I've had people come up to me and say hello by name and I don't even know who they are. It's disturbing to have people know you and you don't know them. It makes the town seem too small. You get too close to people. In some respects it's good, you get to know people and you can help them with their problems, but once I had a hard time. I guess I had arrested somebody or written out a complaint, and their mother called my mother, and she came down on me, and this other person wouldn't talk to her, and it got all mixed up in my family life. With the town being so small you have no place to relax. You go in to buy groceries someplace or have a cup of coffee and you hear people gossiping, saying all kinds of bitter things, and you know the moment you leave they're talking about you. I get anxious. Work is like a time bomb on this job. You have responsibilities. Things come up out of nowhere, it seems, problems, and you have to solve them and you can't afford to be wrong. You stop a car for speeding, it could be a routine thing, although they always say there is no such thing as a routine traffic stop, but say you pull somebody over, speeding, or a taillight out, that car could be stolen, or the person driving it or one of the passengers could be wanted somewhere. You have no way of telling. I've recovered stolen cars on plain traffic stops. Matter of fact, one night the sergeant and I got two. One out of Provincetown and another out of Providence, Rhode Island. We stopped one of them for no taillights, I think, and the other one I forget, but something small. I don't suppose that will ever happen again, but you never know. One night we had a high-speed chase. I forget who I was with but there was a guy taking a leak by the side of the road, and we pulled up and he jumped in his car and took off. Come to find out when we finally stopped it that one of the passengers was wanted for armed robbery. You don't know. When someone splits there's no way of telling why they do. I never like to get put in that position.

"I enjoy this job a lot, and if I left it I would miss it. I don't know what else I'd do. I would miss the excitement. The only thing I'd leave it for, I'd stay in law enforcement, but I would get a specialty, investigation or drugs, where that was all you did, and not ninety thousand other things."

The chief once asked Billy to call the Philadelphia police department. The selectmen wanted information on a Philadelphia man who intended to buy a restaurant in town. I listened in on the other extension with Billy's permission. He dialed City Hall.

The first person he reached placed him on hold, and then an operator came on the line.

"Hello, this is Officer Brooks at the Wellfleet PD up here on the Cape."

"I can't hear you," the voice said, and broke the connection.

Billy called again.

"City Hall, may I help you?"

"Yes, may I have the police department, please."

"What precinct?"

"The police department'll do."

"Yes, but what precinct would you like?"

"Well, ah, downtown'll be all right."

"Philadelphia Police, Metropolitan Division. Sergeant Brock."

"Hello, this is Officer Brooks in Wellfleet up here on the Cape. We want to get a records check on a Philip Adalano who lives in your town. He wants to buy a business up here. Have you got anything on him?"

"Just a minute, I'll give you Records."

Billy tapped a pencil on the table.

"Records, Sergeant Wessler."

"Hello, this is Officer Brooks up here at the Wellfleet PD on the Cape. We'd like a records check on a Philip Adalano who lives in your town. Do you have a file on him?"

Pause.

"Who's this?"

"This is Officer Brooks of the Wellfleet PD on the Cape."

"The Cape?"

"Cape Cod . . . Massachusetts."

Pause.

"What is it you want?"

"We'd like a records check on Philip Adalano, who lives in your town."

"You know where?"

"Not exactly. Just somewhere in the town."

"You have a date of birth, Social Security number?"

"No."

Pause.

"Who is this again?"

"This is Officer Brooks of the Wellfleet police department in Massachusetts. We want a records check on a Philip Adalano. He wants to buy a restaurant here. We wondered if you had any information on him."

"All right. Hold on a minute."

A Sergeant Vandermay came back.

"About this Philip Adalano," he said, "we got nothing on him."

"Nothing?"

"Nope."

"Not even a parking ticket? A red light? Something like that?"

"Not a thing."

"Well, does anyone there in the station have any personal knowledge of him?"

"*What?*"

"I said, does anyone around there in the station know him?"

Pause.

"*Who is this?*"

"The guy's name is Philip Adalano, and—"

"No, who are you?"

"This is Officer Brooks at the Wellfleet PD up here on Cape Cod."

"No, Officer Brooks, no one around here knows him."

"All right. Thank you."

"Not at all."

Billy replaced the receiver on its cradle and said to the dispatcher, "If the Philadelphia PD ever calls here, put them on hold."

8.

Joe Hogan, who for three years had been a member of the Metropolitan Police Force in Washington, D.C., before coming to Wellfleet, used to look out for me, and I relied on him. One night early in the summer he drove me down a deserted road by the ocean and pulled the car to the shoulder. "Anybody told you how to make traffic stops yet?"

"Not really. I've made a few with Paul and some with Billy, but nobody has really said anything about what to do."

"Well, now's the time to learn," he said. "Any time a cop doesn't know what he's getting into, which is a traffic stop, he's in trouble. That's when he can get hurt. You have to be very, very leery all the time. The type of car, sometimes it's a giveaway. You see an LTD wagon, with a guy and a wife and some kids, you figure it's okay. You see a beat-up old Chevy with a couple of teenagers in it, you know it's just circumstance, but you react differently."

He turned off the engine. "When you've got it in your head that you want to stop somebody, you want to find a place to do it. If it's nighttime, follow him until you can pick a spot under a light—always give yourself the edge. Put on the blue lights. If he doesn't see them, give him a shot on the siren. When you get him pulled over, leave the front of the cruiser sticking out toward the road a bit. That puts the engine block in between him and you, in case you need it. Aim the spotlight right in his rear-view mirror. Does two things: a) lights up the car so you can see him, and b) he can't look into his mirror to watch you. He can't see what you're up to."

Joe had me get out of the car with him. We walked ten feet behind it and then turned and faced it. "If you're driving," Joe said, "take the left side of the car, and let your partner take the passenger's. Grab a flashlight, if it's night, and always, *always* unstrap your gun." He did that and began moving forward. "Walk up to the car. Now, sometimes a guy will pull the cruiser up so close behind the other car that you can't even see the license plate. Probably a mistake, you want some distance. It gives you a little time to plan. *Never* get between the two cars. E*spe*cially if you're alone. All the guy has to do is reverse it and bang you right up against the hood, and you're gone. That happened to a guy on the D.C. force when I worked there and I always remembered it.

"Now, if you've got a partner, walk up to the car together and keep your eyes open." We walked forward and stopped at the driver's window. "Tell the driver what you want. Something like 'Good evening, sir, I stopped you because I clocked you at sixty miles per hour in a forty-five zone,' not 'Give me your goddam license, where's the fire?' because he may just *tell* you where the fire is. Now, it may not happen to you, but I was scared to death the first traffic stop I made, and it was for some *small* traffic violation. But you don't know what he's thinking, and you don't know what he's been through that day. He may *very* well have lost his job; he may have gone home and had his wife say, 'Split, I'm divorcing your ass'; he may have found out he's being sued; and he may have gone out and gotten smoked, half-drunk, and he goes through a red light, doesn't see it, probably, and here comes rinky-dink Joe Hogan going to tell him, 'You have to slow up for that goddam red light,' and that is the point right there where he breaks and the next thing you know, *bango!*

"So be careful. Be courteous, when it's to your advantage. Now, if you have the passenger's side, you should be checking out the back seat and the passengers. If you think they stuffed something under the seat, take a look. You can do that. The traffic stop is the one place where the policeman should always be in control of the situation. You have a car with five or six people in it, you know, you don't want five or six people walking around. If you want the driver out, you tell the driver to get out. You got all this?"

"I think so."

"All right. You tell the driver to get out, *always* the passengers will get out, or somebody in the back seat will want to get out, and that's when it goes from being—even if it's something as simple as running a red light, when they all start wanting to climb out—that's when it goes from being nice and cooperative and trying to be professional about it to something else. Then you have to say 'Back in the car' or 'Sit down, I'm not talking to you.' And once it gets to that point, then you get the attitude. You know, it's either 'I'm sorry, Officer, sure I'll get back in the car,' or it'll be 'Why not, what the hell, I can get out if I want to,' something like that. Then you've got problems. If you're alone, you've *really* got problems. You can handle one person, but you can't handle six or seven when they're getting out and roaming around behind you and you can't see what they're doing.

"But forget about that for the moment. Let's say you have a partner, and you're on the passenger's side. If the driver goes into the glove box for his registration, you should be going in there after him. Follow him right in there, shine your light in. Could be drugs in there, could be a needle, could be a gun. If there *is* a gun, you might not always see it."

Then he told me a story that had taken place in Washington. Late at night, driving alone in the cruiser, he heard a bulletin giving the description of a rape suspect, who was Black, and remembered that a few minutes before, he had passed a parked pickup truck with a Black man at the wheel. He remembered where it was and drove by it again. The man appeared to be asleep, and though he looked like he might fit the description, it was too dark for Joe to be certain.

"Twenty minutes later," he said, "this is about three-thirty now, I drive by and he's still there. So I stopped to get a better look at him. In the back of my mind I didn't think that this man was the fellow that committed the crime. He was in the wrong part of town and I didn't think he'd had time to get that far from the scene. But this is thirty-five minutes after I got the call. So I had plenty of time to say to myself by way of preparation if I *do* stop to talk to this guy I'm going to be careful because maybe this bastard just went in and raped somebody, and I forgot to tell you there was a gun mentioned. So, pulled the cruiser di*rec*tly up in front of him, got out of the car, walked up and banged on the door. 'Hey, what're you doing?' He rolls his window down. 'Ah, Jeez, I'm trying to get home,' he says. 'I had a couple to drink, and I didn't want to drive.' I said, 'Where you been?' and he said, 'Ah, I been here and there,' blah, blah. So I'm looking at him, and I start to say to myself *looks like him*, same type of hairdo, mustache, or whatever. So I said, 'C'mon, I'm going to have somebody take a look at you.' So I *yanked* him out of the truck, *threw* him in the back of the cruiser, and off we went. It's him, right, no question about it, it's him. Go back. In the front seat, under*neath* the felt hat with the feathers, right, the pimp that he was, was a thirty-eight Smith and Wesson. Six rounds. Mistake number one: pulled up in *front* of him. Mistake number two: *never* called and told the dispatcher where I was. Mistake number three: never unbuttoned my pistol, never had my hand on it. Mistake number four: very *rudely* went up there and rapped on the door. And number five: never searched him or frisked him, just threw him in the back of the cruiser."

Though these might be mistakes, generally speaking, in this case they turned out not to be. After the trial, Joe went and sought the man out.

"'Would you have shot me?' I said to him. 'I'm asking you honestly, would you have shot me?' The guy said, 'I want to tell you something, brother. You had me by surprise. If you'd come up to that window any other way than you did, you were gone. I would have left you lying in the road.' Do I lose any sleep over that? You bet your ass I do.

"But about your normal traffic stop. You might find you have something else going. You're talking to the driver. Maybe he doesn't have his registration, or maybe the ignition's popped, or maybe you just got a bulletin and you *know* the car's stolen, or maybe you see a gun. Any one of these things. But if it's the case that you *do* see a gun, yell it out to your partner and drop back to the cruiser." Joe took a few steps back to the car, the change jingling in his pants pocket. Reaching in, he pressed the lever releasing the shotgun and pulled it out. "Pick up the mike, grab the shotgun, and kneel behind the door for cover." He dropped to his knees and balanced the gun on the door jamb. "This, by the way, is why you have the engine block between you. Not many guns will go through that. Now, you tell the driver you want his hands out the window where you can see them, passengers' too. If they don't do it, or if they hesitate, pick up the mike again, and say you have the shotgun on his head, and you're going to blow it off if he doesn't hurry up. This is no time to be genteel." He rose from his crouch, took a few steps back, and walked toward the rear of the cruiser, using it as an imaginary car he had stopped. Pulling open the doors, he said, "You then get each guy out of the car and down on the ground with his hands over his head. Say 'I want you over there, and *you* there, and *you* over here.' If you want to, you can cuff them."

I liked making traffic stops. It was something to do when I was bored. I met people, and I found if I was friendly they generally were too. Except for a short period when I was angry at the chief and the sergeant and didn't know enough not to take it out on other people, I rarely gave tickets. Occasionally I was entertained. One night when I was working with Billy he stopped a station wagon on Route 6 because it had no taillights. The car pulled to the shoulder and out of it streamed more young, short, athletic-looking men than there was any explanation for. They jabbered at Billy in a language neither of us understood. He said, *"Boned-jewer,"* and they paused and looked at one another and back at him and he said, "Guess that's not it." There was one woman with them who spoke English and could interpret, and through her Billy was able to get the car's registration and the license from the driver. The registration was from Florida and had expired. The license was from Hungary, also expired. "Hungary?" Billy said. The woman explained that the man had meant to have both the license and the registration renewed but hadn't had a chance to because he had been traveling. "Oh, Jesus," Billy said. "What are they doing here, anyway?"

"These are the acrobats, or most of them, from Ringling Brothers' circus. The circus is in Boston, and they had twenty hours off and they wanted to see Cape Cod and Provincetown because they hear so much about it."

"The circus!" Billy said. "Have they got any extra tickets?"

The woman asked them. "Not with them, but they told me that if you would come to Boston tomorrow they will get you in."

"I can't do that. I have to work. But tell them to be *care-ful*. If they get in an accident with an expired registration and an out-of-date license they're in real trouble, and I'd be in trouble, too, for having let them go."

They were grateful. The woman said her license was valid and she would drive. When they left, Billy said, "Hungary? Where the hell is *that*?"

Until I had my lesson from Joe, I never understood that I was in any danger. About the same time, however, the chief told me this story:

"One day, eight-fifteen in the morning, I'm heading by the medical center, coming to work. There's a car parked off the side of the road, with a couple of real small kids in it. I stopped and asked if I could give them a hand. 'No, the car's stalled,' they said, 'no problem.' 'Well, let me see your license and registration,' I said. The license said the boy was seventeen. He didn't have the registration. He said it was his sister's car. 'I want to check on the sister's car,' I said. 'Shut the engine off.' He reaches under the dashboard and pulls apart two wires. 'Hey, this car's stolen,' I said, and the other kid says, 'No.' I was looking right at him and it looked like a girl. I asked, 'How old are you, miss?' He said he was a boy, but he was so small. There's no danger there, I thought. So I went back to the cruiser, and the dispatcher checks the registration, and it comes back stolen. I walked up, got them out of the car, and said, 'C'mon, boys, you're under arrest. Just follow me.' I didn't think too much of it. It's eight-fifteen in the morning.

"Well, later, at the gas station where they towed the car, the attendant found a hole in the seat with padding over it. There's a gun underneath it, and there's another under the front seat. Both loaded. Each kid could have controlled one. Fifteen and seventeen years old. They were small kids, didn't even look their ages, but they were escapees from a boys' home in Boston."

After that, everyone in a car looked like a criminal to me. Especially men and especially at night. Sometimes when I was alone, and had to stop a car or a van—vans were the worst because you could never see what was going on inside them—I had to force myself to do it. Other times I followed it into Eastham or Truro and called them for a backup. More than a few times I let them go altogether. Once I walked up to a car with my hand resting on the butt of my pistol and caught myself at it and felt frightened and just said, "Forget it," to the driver. I sat in the cruiser afterward and thought of something Chickie had recently told me. "We get blamed for coming on too strong," he said. "You walk up to a car and you get rowdy, and they say, 'What are you getting so rough for?' You can't explain it to them. Fear is always there. You just have to learn to live with it, because if you lose that edge you'll get hurt, sooner or later."

The FBI periodically issued bulletins to local police departments. The chief collected them in a notebook, which he left on a desk in the station. I found it by accident, when I was looking for something to read. Several bulletins covered ways in which policemen had been injured or killed while making traffic stops. There were obvious ones—run over, shot by the driver or a passenger who held a gun—and less obvious ones. Some had been shot by motorcyclists who concealed in their handlebars guns that used shotgun shells. The bulletin warned against facing the ends of any handlebars. Another cautioned against guns concealed in car doors and trunk lids. I read them all twice, hoping to absorb the information.

The most recent one said drug addicts had been placing contaminated needles between the seats of cars, where policemen run their hands while making searches. Several patrolmen had scratched themselves unwittingly and contracted hepatitis, and by the time the FBI had caught on to it some of them had died.

9.

Paul Francis

"IN THE FIRST six months, I didn't like being a cop. I was too sensitive to other people's feelings and what they might think about me. I had just come back from New Mexico, where I was in the service. The only reason I came back was I was a homesick child. I could have stayed there; my wife and I thought about it and we could have made it in New Mexico, but I wanted to come back. Lonely. I took this job, but I didn't want to. It seemed a little stupid-sounding to me, being a cop, but there was money involved, more money than I was making. It didn't take too long for me to like it, though. I don't know, really, what changed, except I guess I just matured. That was three years ago, and since then I haven't ever really wanted to change professions. I wouldn't quit anyway because I couldn't afford to. I wouldn't know where the hell to begin. I don't have anything for a backup. There's no job I could do other than being a policeman. I can't go into computers, or school-teaching, or anything like that. I could go fishing, I suppose. I know about that, since I was old enough to walk I fished summers on and off with my father, but I don't like to fish, and I don't want to fish. I really don't like it. Besides, this job is challenging to me. It's your wit against another guy's in a lot of cases, whether you can catch him doing something wrong and how you can sneak up on him. It's a challenge to me to take a two-hundred-pound guy, or a six-foot guy, cuff him, lock him up, take him to jail, and say that little old five-foot-seven me put him there. Not so much the power it took as the fact that I caught him doing something wrong and I took him in. If we had armed robberies, that would be more exciting for me, I guess, give me a chance to pull the gun.

"This job is interesting, too. You're always seeing weird things. One time Charlie Valli and me just left my house and we had ice cream cones. It was Fourth of July. We were sitting there licking our cones, and we saw a car. 'Jesus Christ, I guess we got to check this out,' I said. We got out, and we both looked at the same time, and we both knew what was going on. 'Son of a bitch,' I said. 'This guy's screwing.' I ran up to one side and Charlie ran up to the other side, and this guy's screwing the life out of this girl, and I'm licking at my cone, and Charlie's got his arms folded on the passenger's side, and I'm tapping at the window, and I say, 'Hey, what're you doing?' The guy looks up.

'Jesus Christ,' he says, 'nothing like getting caught with your pants down.' I said, 'Show me your license, I want to make sure you're married to this girl.' Then she asked me to turn around, and I said, 'Lady, we've seen everything now. We got you cold turkey.' They never saw Charlie and he stood there while I was supposed to be turning my back. They jumped a foot when he finally spoke up.

"That's the funny stuff. Other times you say to yourself, *'How the hell can people live like this?'* Nobody ever calls you when they're behaving themselves. As a rule, you always get called when people are at their worst. It's sad. It depresses me. But it helps me in the respect that I know I don't want to be like that. I understand myself better because I see how I don't want to be. I don't want to go out drinking and smoking marijuana and getting smelly drunk all the time. I don't go out to barrooms because then you get in trouble with other people's wives. I get in enough trouble just by the rumors that go around." He had just separated from his wife—it turned out temporarily—and was being gossiped about. "Whatever these people do, I try to avoid. I just want to do this job the best I can, and not get hurt while I'm doing it. I've already come to the conclusion after the incidents we've had, especially the Crowley arrest, that I'm not going to do it easy anymore. If a guy swings at me, the guy's going down. I don't care how he goes down, he's going down. Not shoot him, of course. Self-defense-wise I'm going to hit him, that's all there is to it. Knock him down and throw him in the car and hope you have a good case. Sometimes that doesn't matter. You could lose the case anyway, even if it's a good one. I lost one one time because the lawyer said I didn't identify the defendant, didn't point him out in the courtroom. I got bullshit over that because I *did* point him out. After that kind of thing happens, though, I don't really give a damn. I don't really care. The only thing that bothers me is that I didn't present a good enough case to get him convicted. When I lose, I'm lodging in my mind how I'm going to present the next one. With each time I find out something new, and each time my record gets better. I remember what to say, and what not to say. I just do my job at the time. I get the man off the street and take him to jail, and if the judge sees fit to let him go, well, he sees it the way he sees it.

"It's a bitch of a job, though, sometimes. Any job is hard on a person. I don't think this is the hardest, but it's one of them. This job just breaks you all around. Tears you up one side and down the other. It breaks *you* up, it breaks your wife, breaks your family, everyone around you. Whether you're in uniform or not you're an asshole to everyone. Someone can even *call* me an asshole, and I can't do anything about it. Christ, in the old days somebody would give a cop a hard time and he'd slap them upside the head. Can't do that now. Police brutality. I have to smile and walk by. You can't have pride in yourself, or hold it publicly because you get in trouble if you defend it. Sometimes I think it would be better if I moved out of town. I don't socialize with anyone as it is. I like to be with people, but it usually has to be people I know, people who know me, so they understand me. It may be the job, it may be my own problem, I don't know. They *say* it's the police job, but I'd probably be the same anyway. Over my whole life I only had one real friend, and he moved away, and he has a wife and kids on his own now. I keep it all to myself, and I guess my wife takes the brunt of it. I spend a lot of time by myself. I work out, lift weights. I read anything I can get my hands on about Zen. I try to understand it. I *try*, I should try harder. If I did, I know it would come. I can't exactly put my finger on what *it* is, but I know it, if you understand. I don't believe there's anything supernatural about life. There's no God that created us and put us here, and we have to worship. My theory is that we're just vegetables planted here in this garden, and some UFOs come and check us out and see how we're doing. We're just an experiment for another planet, which is all it probably amounts to. Zen is just a word. It represents the thing itself. They have commandments, you're not supposed to have any ego, no lust, desires, not supposed to want material things—you wonder how you exist not wanting material things, but people do, if they're in the right state of mind. You could probably function better in police work if you were in a state of enlightenment. Anyway, it's something I don't understand yet, but I have an idea about. In Zen, as I understand it, there's nothing to figure out, yet you have to figure it out. It's not as much that you gain anything, it's that you get rid of everything else to see it. You have to keep an open mind. If your mind is clouded with thoughts and prejudices you can't learn anything. If they had a monastery around here I'd go and try it. Probably learn something. Probably get stiff legs and a sore back.

If my wife ever left me I think that's what I'd do, I'd go to Japan and go to a monastery. I'd hate like hell to do it, I mean my ego would, I'd think how are you going to live without all these material things that seem so important to you, but I know you can.

"Before becoming a police officer I was a timid and shy person, maybe a pessimist, I don't know, but anyway I opened up more. I'm not afraid of people like I used to be. The police job wakens you to how minds work, how you think people are so complicated, how you see people walking down the road, and you look at them and you say, 'Gee, looks like a complicated person.' But when you set them under a police situation, people are so much the same that you think about your own problems and desires, lusts and apprehensions, stuff like that, you feel them in yourself, and then when you finally see these people actually showing their emotions, you see they're not any better than you are."

10.

AT TIMES, ROUTE 6, between Orleans and Wellfleet, is four lanes, undivided; or three lanes, with the middle lane available sometimes to both directions for passing; or two lanes, with a combination of straight and broken lines that allow passing by turns to one direction, then the other, and on straightaways to both. In stretches where it is three lanes, a person wanting to turn across traffic must either stop in his own lane and risk being hit from behind, or move to the middle lane and take his chances. I once saw a head-on collision between a car waiting in the middle lane to turn and one that had pulled out without seeing the other blocking his way. I have also seen cars hit from behind in the middle lane. In spots the road has been painted and restructured so often, and old lines so inadequately blacked over, that it is difficult for a stranger to know with any confidence whether he is in the breakdown lane, the travel lane, or the passing lane. In the summer this road is almost always incredibly congested and there is competition for the passing lane, with the occasional result of what police call "fatals."

I can't imagine a more dangerous road for high-speed chases, yet they were reasonably frequent—once a month, perhaps, and more often in the summer.

Cars were sometimes stolen in Provincetown, reported missing, and spotted in Wellfleet, and chases ensued. They were very stimulating affairs. Speaking of a highspeed chase, Paul said, "If it's a long chase I get nervous. The longer they are, the more scared you get, but the more persistent you get. You think, *That son of a bitch, he ain't no different from me. I'm going to get him.* You don't think about your life at the time. Every now and then it will flash through your mind and you will think, *What the hell am I doing? Am I crazy?* But you keep going, you keep driving because there's something pushing you, you started something and you got to finish it. Even if I don't write that son of a bitch up, just to say that I stopped him, that he didn't get away, is enough."

Joe told me about a chase that involved him and two cars stolen from the same man.

"It was Sunday morning," he said, "midnight-to-eight, and I had just been up to the coffee shop and had a cup of java and I'm driving along Route Six, half asleep, waiting for the shift to end, and *bang*, out they come, Will Colgan's truck and his Monte Carlo, out the driveway like a bastard. The truck sees me and goes *screeeech*, and does a complete turn-around right in the middle of Route Six,

and heads up the road towards Eastham with the Monte
Carlo right after him. I knew the truck was stolen as soon
as it came out of the driveway, but I thought Will was in
the Monte Carlo chasing the guy who stole his truck. So
I'm trying to see who it is at the wheel, and I went right
by him because I had the speed, and it's not Will. And
then right about that time the dispatcher's on, and she
says he called and said both his cars were stolen. So I said,
'Well, you can't do that in *my* town, asshole,' and I zing up
beside the Monte Carlo, and he went off the road into the
gift shop parking lot that's just past Will's driveway. I'm
chasing the truck down the road, and I call three-seven-
six, the county radio shack, to get in touch with Eastham.
Jock, the guy who works midnight-to-eights down there,
was on. He says, 'A thousand good mornings,' like he always does, and here I am at ninety miles an hour chasing
this goddam truck and I say, 'Three-seven-six, emergency,
this is Charlie One.' 'Thousand good mornings to you,' he
says. 'Hey, *Jock*! I'm chasing a car up Route Six towards
Eastham, advise Eastham cruiser.' And he says, 'Okay.'
So he calls them and they're waiting as we go through
the traffic lights. They're *way* off to the side of the road. I
guess they have a policy there: if they're coming through,
get the hell out of the way 'cause they'll kill you. And this
crazy son of a bitch is *really* going. What he does is he
lets me catch up to him, and then he slams on his brakes,
and I'd have to slam my brakes on too. So he did this two
times, and I got the drift, you know, so I eased back and let
him go. Then what the crazy bastard does is he goes into
the other lane, the northbound lane, and he's forcing traf-

fic into *my* lane, so I have to swing around and get on the other side too. I'm sweating blood by now. If I'd had any smarts at all, because Orleans was already notified and they were waiting at the traffic circle, I would have backed off and said that's it. Lights off, siren off, and just continued down the road until I see him racked up against a tree, or he gets stopped at the rotary. But pride, you know.

"So Jock comes on the radio and he says, 'How're you doing?' And I say, 'I'm almost at the rotary, Jock,' and he says, 'Let's hope he doesn't know it's there.' And he *didn't* know it was there, either. He comes up to it at full tilt and I get up on his tail and start pushing. He can't stop now because he's got the rotary coming. He doesn't know it's there, but he sees the woods in the middle of it and he knows *some*thing's wrong. If he had stopped then, we would have smacked. But he went right up over the edge"—there are some stones that form a kind of curb to the inside of the rotary—"hit the grade right on at about sixty-five. Almost flipped, but he straightened out. And I didn't time it right either because I went up over the goddam thing too. Blew the tire right out of the cruiser. When he hit, though, his door opened and his butt flew out, and he's holding on to the wheel, sitting out in the air and trying to drive the truck. So he lets go and goes rolling in the grass, and I went right across the grass and back out onto the road. And I'm savage, Sunday morning, blew the tire out of the car. So I grab my gun and go running across the grass. *Hold it right there, you son of a bitch!* and, Jesus, next thing I know he's into the roughage there in the middle of the rotary. So we call up and get the dog.

By this time there's cops everywhere from Brewster and Orleans. There's a state trooper there, too. The dog officer shows up, I go over to my cruiser and get on the loud-speaker. Now what I didn't know was we'd woken up everyone at the motel overlooking the rotary with the siren. All the people were out on the balconies in their pajamas and bathrobes, watching us yelling and running around and carrying on like fools. So I get on the loudspeaker. 'All right,' I said, 'this is the police.' Like he didn't know. 'C'mon out of there.' He's not coming out. So the dog goes in, and we trail after him. The trooper's in there, and it's muddy as hell, it's a marsh, you know, and as soon as we got in it we sank right up to our knees. Well, the trooper's bullshit—spit-shine boots and all that. 'If I catch that miserable son of a bitch,' he said, 'I'll put a bullet through his head.' So he wanders off with another cop, and I go another way, and I find the guy laying up in a bush, all scratched because he had no shirt. I said, 'You're under arrest.' 'What for?' 'For stealing a car.' 'I didn't steal no car. I been here all night. Got drunk and come in here and slept.' I walked him across the road up into the cruiser and suddenly everyone up there in the balconies at the motel breaks into applause."

I WAS A passenger in two high-speed chases, both of them in my first month. While they were on, I had no expectation of surviving them. The first happened as a result of a call from Eastham. "A car is heading into your town at a high rate of speed." Eastham was always saying that. Perhaps they had a department no-chase rule, because I can't count the number of times, at all hours, that I got that call from them. On this occasion it was dusk. Paul was driving. When we got the call he parked the car in the lot of a gas station by the side of the highway, far enough off the road to be concealed by the station's tire display. We waited. The engine idled. I was too green to know that though chases weren't rare, they didn't happen every week, and anyway there were eight men to divide them among, which meant that if there was, say, one chase a month, the odds were that over a certain period of time not every man would have participated in one—and that made each chase more dangerous, for the driver's lack of practice.

Long before the car arrived, we heard it. Joe said once, "You know, you hear these things, especially at night, about five miles away, and by the time they get up to you you're *all* worked up. Could be a truck, could be a *plane*, you don't know *what* the hell it is."

After two or three minutes, the car, a gold and black sixties GTO, passed us, apparently without noticing we were there, and Paul pulled out after it. It took us only seconds to get on the road, but by the time we had speed, the car was out of sight, a quarter of a mile ahead on the far side of a rise. Paul's foot on the accelerator was pressed to the floor. From a dead stop we were nearly even after about three quarters of a mile and had clocked the car at eighty-six. We were on a two-lane section of the road, and when Paul passed a car on a curve going uphill, I looked for the seat belt. It was tangled between the door and the seat. Paul saw me working to free it and said, "Don't bother, you'll only get your gun frigged up in it." Paul had on the blue lights. The driver ignored them and the siren, too.

We entered a three-lane stretch, approaching a bend. Our direction was confined to single file, but the other two lanes, going south, could pass. The car pulled left over the yellow line into approaching traffic—two cars in the far lane braked—and overtook one car and then another before pulling back so abruptly that the body of the car tipped and settled against the frame. All of this took place at great speed in less than five seconds. Paul pulled out after the car. The wind poured through my window. "Shut that thing," Paul yelled. "I can't hear the radio." He was leaning toward the speaker, driving with one hand and holding the radio mike in his right. We were going ninety. Someone was talking—I couldn't hear it well—but it was a man's voice, and not that of Myra, our dispatcher. Two cars, hearing the siren, braked and pulled off the road in front of us. We went by them so fast that I couldn't see any faces, but the man driving the first car had his shoulders hunched as if against an attack from behind. In our lane a car approached—our combined speed perhaps one hundred and forty—and then swerved right and off the road. Paul jerked us back into the right lane. "*This crazy son of a bitch is going to get us killed!*" he shouted. The car passed again. We followed at over ninety to cut the lead. I looked down at my body; my legs and feet were pressed rigidly to the floor, and I realized I would never survive a crash at this speed. I looked at Paul, leaning forward, one hand gripping the wheel and the other holding the mike, and saw he was absorbed. (Later, when I chased someone, I realized that from the driver's vantage a chase is bracing, and under the right conditions—particularly a dry road—entirely without the terror the helpless passenger feels.) We were at around ninety still, close enough to the other car so that if he struck anything we couldn't prevent ourselves from following. The car crossed into Truro, and a man in the back seat turned three-quarters profile and looked at us, perhaps to see if we had followed. In the glow from our roof lights his face was quickly blue, then not, then blue again. He looked scared. The other person in the back seat turned. The car began to slow and then pulled over. Paul called in the stop, and a Truro cruiser, already alerted by our dispatcher, arrived with lights flashing, made a U-turn, and pulled up behind us. Paul was out the door and I was reaching for my door handle when I heard him say, "Holy shit, it was a *girl*."

She approached us, apologized, and said she hadn't seen us and was in a hurry to get to Provincetown. One of the two men with her was a transvestite, in a low-cut black dress and gold sandals. The Truro cop was talking to them and I went over and listened to their conversation. "What are you doing in that dress?" the cop said.

"We're going dancing."

"You're a faggot?"

"Yes."

"You go to bed with men?"

"Yes."

"And you don't mind?"

"No."

"Ugh, that's disgusting."

The girl came back to the car with a ticket bearing a list of violations, including "operating to endanger." It is a serious charge, one on which it is difficult to win a conviction, but Paul did.

THE LAST PERSON I would have picked to be driven by in a chase was Billy. And I couldn't put my finger on why until one night when he said, "When it comes to chases, I don't get scared, I just get excited."

At two A.M., a week after my chase with Paul, Billy and I were driving Route 6 in South Wellfleet, where we had done some door checks, and wanted now to go to the Lighthouse. Billy turned the car around and reached for the restaurant key, which usually hung on the directional signal lever, but now wasn't there. Paul, who was off at two, had just dropped the other cruiser at the chief's house so the chief could drive it to work in the morning. Paul had been in the Lighthouse earlier, and we stopped at the chief's to see if he had left the key in the car. We looked but didn't find it. Billy called the station to see if Paul had left. The dispatcher said he had, but only just, and that we could probably catch him on the highway.

Paul's route home passed the chief's driveway, off Route 6, so we parked there and waited. Headlights appeared, and when they passed and we saw Paul's car, Billy pulled out after them. He drew even with Paul and motioned for him to pull over. Paul accelerated. Billy accelerated and put on the blue lights. Paul accelerated. "Come on, Paul, will you," Billy said. He turned on the wig-wags and punched the manual siren button. There was a rumble at the low end of the siren's range. We were within two miles of the chief's house, and if we had woken him when we went for the key, which was likely, he would hear us now. *What if he asks us in the morning what we were up to last night*, I thought.

There was no other traffic. Paul was traveling about seventy, now in the middle lane, now in the right, trying to block us whenever Billy attempted to pass, and it was nearly two more miles before we had a straightaway and the middle lane. Billy drew even with him. I rolled down the window and was about to shout "*Key*," when I was distracted by headlights approaching. Billy saw them too, and he pulled back before I had a chance to say anything to Paul. The lights passed and I turned to follow them out of sight. Instead of continuing, they slowed, turned, and doubled back. "Who the hell is that?" I said.

"Who's who?"

The car was drawing fast on us and I said, "Those headlights," when a blue light flashed on and a state police car overtook us. He drew even with Paul, braked, and swerved wildly toward him. "Oh, shit," Billy said. When he was nearly touching Paul's car, the trooper pulled back. Then he pulled left, preparing to swerve again, and this time I was sure he'd hit Paul, to force him over, but Paul braked and pulled to the side. The trooper cut in front of us, immediately behind Paul, and was out of the car with his gun unstrapped before Billy and I had our hands on our doors.

"Oh, Jesus," Billy said. Paul stepped from his car. He was, of course, in uniform.

"What the *hell's* going on here?" the trooper said. Billy talked up to them, but I stayed back by the car. I was sure we'd made a very bad mistake, and once the trooper talked to the chief, the three of us would be on midnights.

Billy and the trooper had a moment's conversation, which I couldn't hear. The trooper stood with his knees locked and his feet spread shoulder width. I saw Paul reach into his pocket and hand Billy the Lighthouse key. I heard Billy ask the trooper if he'd like to come for coffee. The trooper declined. The trooper and Paul left. Billy came back to the car. He looked shaken.

"What'd he say?" I asked.

"That's Patsy Farrel," Billy said. "I heard he killed a man once. Ran him over."

THERE WAS FOR a time a white Thunderbird, with an unlit license plate, that would drive through town on the highway and try to enlist the police in a chase. Eastham wrecked a cruiser in one of them, and Paul and Chickie said they were up to a hundred and ten one night before they lost him.

Joe also chased him one night. "I was parked up at Rookie's Pizza, on Route Six," he told me. "This is about two in the morning, summertime, and this car comes into town, and he was going like a bitch. Screaming down the road. All I saw was white and taillights. Off I go after him north toward Truro. I'm slowly catching up so at least I have his taillights in sight, and by the time we got to Davis' corner, which is tight, you know, if you have any speed, I was pretty close to him. I could see what kind of car it was, T-bird, so I knew who I was dealing with. I was just getting ready to call in and tell Truro I got him. I have the mike in my hand. There was no way this bastard could turn off at the speed he's going. If he doesn't buy it at Davis' corner, then I'll get him because I know what speed to take it at. Well, I don't know how he did it, but he got around Davis' corner and hooked a right on Lecount Hollow Road. And I never expected him to do that. It's practically impossible. I see him do it, and I try to turn, but my microphone cord wraps around the steering wheel and the mike flies out of my hand, and the tires are screeching, and I'm trying not to hit the telephone pole at the intersection. So I lost him. Called Truro and they couldn't find him. Jesus Christ, I don't know how he *ever* made that turn."

A DIARY EXCERPT. Joe Hogan: "If you have to chase somebody any length of distance, you know, if he gives you a good merry-go-round, by the time you get to them, or they decide to stop, you're usually pretty bullshit."

I drove myself in two modest chases, one in winter and the other in spring. The first happened at the end of a long snowstorm. Around seven one morning I was approaching Route 6 from Pamet Point Road, near the Truro border, where I had been looking at animal tracks in the snow. Snow covered the highway so thoroughly that the traffic lines, and even the edges of the road, were hidden. A man was driving a black car down the middle of it, doing fifty where twenty-five was pushing it. Snow blew over the car's hood and roof, and the wheels spread it like a wake. I flicked on the blue-light switch. During the first mile I drove with speed and ignored the feeling I had in my hands, from the wheel, that the car did not seem to be holding the road. During the second mile, going around a bend, I tapped the brakes and lost control of the rear end. It felt suddenly as if there were nothing under my wheels.

At each turn after that I let him pull ahead and waited for the straightaways to recover the distance. After six miles, I drew even. I was only half in the middle lane and the rest in the far lane, with the lights working and the siren sounding, and I pointed for him to pull to the shoulder. He looked at me then accelerated, and passed into Eastham. I gave it up, took down his license-plate number, went back to the station, traced the plate, wrote out a ticket, and sent it to him, certified mail.

The second chase was similar, except that instead of snowing, it had been raining. Again it was early morning. I had been up at the Episcopal church, off the highway, looking around, had decided it was time for breakfast, and was coming down the narrow tree-lined driveway toward Route 6 when a station wagon flew by splashing water. Long chase. I caught him about a mile into Eastham. The whole way I had felt the tires wanting to let loose and skim over the tops of puddles. It had made me very nervous. Later, in court, the man said he had tried to reason with me, but he could see how upset I was, and he didn't think it safe to press it. "I didn't want to get shot," was what he said.

He asked me for a break. I gave him one—I still wonder why—by writing up his speed at something consider-
ably lower than the seventy-five to eighty I had clocked
him at in a forty-five zone.

He contested the ticket at a hearing, lost, had a trial,
lost, appealed, and lost again.

Several months after I had left the job, Joe Hogan, in
uniform, met the man in the Lighthouse. When he asked
about me and Joe said I was in Ireland, the man replied,
"Good goddam place for him. Hope he stays there."

Over coffee Joe learned from the man that the attorney's
bill for the twice-failed defense of a fifteen-dollar speeding
ticket had come to seven hundred and fifty dollars.

11.

Sherman A. Merrill, Jr.

SHERMAN A. MERRILL, Jr., was thirty-two, carried a brief-case, and lived in Provincetown with his parents. His face was round. He had small, clear eyes and thick, widely set eyebrows, like small mustaches. He was not tall. He was overweight and did not look especially strong, but he probably was. He was placid and imperturbable, and I admired that in him, but his temper was ferocious when finally aroused. I often heard how he had manhandled the entire kitchen staff of a restaurant one evening because one of them had pointed a genuine-looking rubber gun at someone. It was the only time anyone had ever seen Sherman angry, and his audience had been impressed.

Sherman had a labored way of speaking. Meaning "When I caught the guy he was speeding," Sherman would say "At the particular point in time when I apprehended the subject, he was operating his vehicle at a high rate of speed." Rather than make a phone call, he "utilized the phone." One evening while we were working together he stopped the car at a gas station and said, "I'll just utilize the Coke machine and then we can get going." On a department report detailing his investigation of a B & E, Sherman once wrote, "Forcible entry does not appear to be present."

Three mornings a week Sherman left Provincetown and drove ninety miles each way to classes at Bridgewater State, where he studied sociology. The other men said, a trifle defensively, that all the book learning in the world couldn't compensate for a lack of street sense. Sherman felt it was important to have both.

"Education gives you a broader outlook," he said. "More knowledge. It enables you to perceive and understand situations better. You need both the theory and the reality. You can utilize the experience and compensate with the theory. Whereas, if you don't have the education working with experience in law enforcement, I would say you're working with a micro sort of situation, as opposed to the macro view of having the education. It's more condensed, and you're not being objective, I should say, about the whole aspect of law enforcement. You isolate yourself to what's happening in your immediate environment. This is a problem you run into and it becomes a bad habit after a while, where you just concentrate on the small aspects of the immediate community. And by no means is law enforcement, or police work, minute. It encompasses quite a bit. You're dealing with self-defense, weapons, and so

forth, you're dealing with the sociological, the psychological, and, obviously, the behavioral sciences. You're dealing
with a managerial type of a level of communication." For
a time Sherman had seriously considered enrolling in a
management training program.

"I like to be prepared," he said. "My résumé is a *solid*
two pages—I'm trying to *keep* it to two—and there's
quality in the résumé. Graduated top third air controllers'
school; top third law-enforcement program, police academy; honors, Burdett College; Dean's List, Cape Cod
Community College, I don't know, *several* times; first in
leadership class in the Navy. There's quality there. I could
go anyplace. Say I got hurt on the job, I could take a desk
job, no problem."

ONE NIGHT WHEN Sherman and I were riding in the
cruiser, someone called the station to report a man apparently drunk, walking unsteadily and weaving into traffic along the edge of Route 6, and we went to pick him
up. On the way, Sherman talked about himself. "To me,
the uniform can at times be a disadvantage," he remarked.
"Because I am not the type of person to use authority. If
you're familiar with the X and Y theory about the managerial approach, I'll go more with the Y than I will with
the X. The X is the strong approach, the authoritarian has
the control, and 'You do as I say.' The Y type of approach,
or theory, deals with working with the individual, and
having good communication, and having him cooperate
because he wants to."

The man walking along Route 6 turned out to be an Irishman, with a thick brogue. Sherman cuffed his hands behind his back and put him in the cruiser, and we set out for Provincetown. The wind blew loudly through the partially open back window, obscuring parts of the conversation.

"Communications is a big factor," Sherman said to me. "If you can't communicate, you're going to have a problem. You're not going to be able to get your thoughts across. You're not going to be able to get the elements of a crime, and so forth. And at times you have to communicate on a sophisticated level to project an image of professionalism. I feel I can relate to people and have a good rapport with them. I don't want to sound conceited here, but I feel as if I'm knowledgeable enough so anyone I come into contact with I can converse."

"What am I being locked up for?" the Irishman in the back seat said.

"For your protection," Sherman said.

"You're protecting me from whom? From whom?"

"From yourself. Making sure that you don't get hurt."

"Jesus, I can defend myself from anybody."

"I'm not saying you can't. But how would you like to get run over by a car while you're out there walking along the road?"

Sherman turned back to me. "After talking with a person for a while, I have a good understanding—as much as one can without going into depth—of what type of person it is. I read them. I've always enjoyed analyzing things psychologically, and a lot of people don't like to be analyzed. You have to do it without their knowing you're doing it. I've had quite a few psychology courses—enough so, not totally, I can have an understanding of an individual's behavior. And now that I'm majoring in sociology and minoring in psychology at Bridgewater, and leaning toward social work, I'm getting both aspects, plus the reality of the job."

The Irishman interrupted from the back seat. "What the hell are you talking about? I'm a man, mister. I'm a man, and you're a man too. Why do you want to hit me with an automobile?"

"Nobody wants to hit you with an automobile, calm down." Sherman went on, "Learning skills exist as far as being able to interpret verbal and nonverbal communication, you know, when to talk, and when not to. So these factors come with experience and also the classroom. Analyze a person? Well, I analyze him afterwards, unless the situation gives me enough time to poke a bit to find out what his strong points and his weaknesses are. I can use that to my advantage, and in the long run to his advantage. And that's what I like to do, to be able to help, and the education prepares me. To me, making a bust is very easy, and it's not the most rewarding part of the job. That's the law enforcement part. I get more enjoyment out of helping than I do out of making a big bust, and I *have* made quite a few of them."

"You said you were going to hit me with an automobile," the Irishman said. "By Jesus, be a man. Knock it off. You have something to say?"

"I don't have anything to say," Sherman replied.

"Who's the other guy?"

"He's observing tonight."

"He's observing. Well, Jesus, he should get some new glasses. He's observing what? What's he observing—you taking me down from Wellfleet?"

"Not only you—"

"*Only me!*"

"*Not* only you. How police function."

"Watch out for those headlights," the Irishman said.

"I know. I saw them."

"I don't want to get killed for zero."

"No, you won't."

"Yeah, but you insulted me, put these handcuffs on me. For what?"

"The handcuffs are standard procedure. We're trying to help you out."

"Trying to help me out? I'm a man, goddammit, which is more than you assholes are."

There was a pause and then Sherman went on.

"I have always been interested in law enforcement," he said. "I think it's from a condition in our society of watching a lot of television, westerns and so forth, war movies, a little masculinity thing. There is power in being a cop. The uniform gives you some. Authority. It's almost the fact that you won't tolerate anything. And the fact that we're basically a violent society, violence is compensating for violence. You have control in the sense that it's visual. With fear. That's the only element of control that exists. You represent authority in a semi-military type of an individual. From the minute you walk into an area, individuals have already been conditioned through past experience, and norms and mores and so forth, that you represent authority and can take someone's freedom away. Actually, it's an implementation of fear. You're carrying your fear with you. Fear for the person, that you may do bodily harm to him, or that you may take his freedom away. And there's not too many individuals in our world that can take somebody's freedom away, and one of them is a police officer. A lawyer can't even take someone's freedom away. A judge can, but a judge doesn't react in the street."

"Anybody got a cigarette there?"

"I don't smoke," Sherman said.

"I didn't ask you that. I said, 'Anybody got a cigarette?' What's the matter? You don't give Irishmen cigarettes? You just break their wrists? What's the charge? What am I charged with?"

"Bein' incapacitated."

"Huh?"

"Bein' incapacitated."

"I can't hear a word you're saying."

"*Bein'* incapacitated."

"*B and E and what?*"

"No, *not* B and E. *Bein'* under the influence of alcohol."

"Wouldn't even give me a cigarette. Jeez, I'll remember that. Goddam Yanks. You went all the way to—where the hell did you go?"

"Wellfleet. That's where you were."

"That's right, all the way there to insult me. You insulted me, mister."

"We're the Wellfleet Police."

"Yeah, well, all right. My back is hurting from these handcuffs."

"We didn't hurt your back."

"You bum."

"I told you not to move them around."

"Not to what?"

"Not to move."

"Not to what? Now you arrested me for what?"

"Incapacitated."

"Incapacitated. Now what in the name of Jesus might that be?"

"Under the influence of alcohol."

"Under the influence of alcohol, huh? Well, I hope you come under the influence of it sometimes. I hope you explain that in court."

"You're not going to court. We're just taking you to Provincetown and you can sleep a few hours and then go home. You live in P-town, right?"

"You're damn right I do. I live there. By Jesus, you better live there, too, mister. Because you're not going to jet away with this. How would you like to be treated like his, sir, with chains on your back. Run over by an automobile."

"That's standard procedure."

"*Standard procedure! It's standard procedure to run somebody over with an automobile?*"

We were by then at the parking lot of the Provincetown police station. Sherman opened the cruiser's back door, and the man climbed out. A Provincetown cruiser stopped to see if Sherman needed a hand. "No, I'm just taking him in," Sherman said. "IP"—meaning intoxicated person. Standing behind the Irishman and holding him by the handcuffs, Sherman pushed him toward the station door. When the man resisted, Sherman grabbed his collar, twisted the cuffs, and gave him the bum's rush.

There was a sergeant on duty at the desk. All the cells were empty; the doors stood open. Sherman and the sergeant frisked the man, emptied his pockets, removed his belt and the handcuffs, and propelled him into the nearest cubby. The sergeant closed the door. We stepped back into the station proper.

"What's the charge?" the Irishman yelled. "I want a charge."

The sergeant walked to the door, opened it, and shouted, "You want a charge? Hold on, I'll go to the garage and get a battery."

When Sherman had filled out the appropriate papers, we left.

On the trip back he was philosophical. "It's the type of job where you see the harsh realities of life," he said. "People passing away, fatal accidents, the emotionally disturbed; it's the harsher realities of life. And you never forget them. But if I had went with the management training program, I'd be staring out the window now in an office somewhere. Here, I'm involved with everything."

12.

NOT ALL MY training took place on the job. Now and then a police department somewhere on the Cape would hold what was called an in-service training session—an hour or two of lecture and discussion, following a film on first aid, or traffic laws, or some other aspect of the work—and I would attend. I spent an evening once with a state trooper whose topic was domestics, family disputes. The trooper's specialty was women, and I learned things that night that I never knew before.

The trooper was a short, sturdy, pudding-faced man, with cropped hair and dark eyes. He addressed us from behind a lectern. "Now, while your majority of arrests you're going to find you don't have any problems with," he said, "women are sometimes definitely going to be a problem. You can simplify this problem for yourself by recognizing some of the possible attitudes of the female prisoner, and knowing the acceptable procedures and the officer's responsibility in dealing with her. As in all parts of the job, your best weapon is preparation.

"Now, a woman's first impulse after she learns you're going to try to arrest her may be to try to change your mind. To accomplish this, she may try any one or more of the following things: one, her personal charm and femininity; two, a tearful bid for sympathy; three, try to impress you with her importance, if she has any, a job or something like that, parents have money; or four, threaten you with the loss of your job. Or five, she may become angry and sullen.

"The best kind of answer to these tactics is courtesy, coupled with an obvious determination to proceed with a lawful arrest.

"When she sees she's being arrested, when she knows you're going to go *through* with it, a woman's attitude may change at any time, without warning. One minute you may find her cooperative and charming, the next she's belligerent and spiteful for no apparent rhyme or reason. These are some of the causes of that change, they're some of the difficulties with women prisoners.

"For a start, a woman is seldom amused by jokes at her own expense. She may be sensitive to real or *imagined* insults—and if she is, even a *casual* remark by an officer may offend her. Give you an example. One night my partner and I—this was back when I was a local, on the force in Haron—we made an arrest after a domestics—two women fighting in a bar over a man—and we went in there, and after a lot of screaming and tussling and scratching we got them apart and put one of them in our cruiser and the other in another car. The woman in our car just sat in the back, quietly, I guess she was tired out, and my partner said, he was only trying to be friendly and loosen things up, he said, 'Boy, you sure got a big yell for such a little woman,' something harmless like that, and she took it the wrong way, and started up all over again, this time with us. This was before I knew what to do. I *should* just have let her yell herself out, but I was trying to reason with her and calm her down. We finally had to stop the car and call for help. You never heard such a racket. She used such bitter profanity I thought it would leave cavities in her teeth. And it was over nothing, so you see what I mean. If you are with a woman prisoner and you have any thoughts, it's probably best you keep them to yourself, at least until she's out of your hands. Keep conversation to a minimum, between you and her, and just to be safe, between you and your partner, if you have one. If you get a woman who likes to talk—and most of them do—and she starts asking a lot of questions, just answer yes or no. Yes, ma'am, no, ma'am. Be polite. Generally speaking, you'll get through the arrest with a minimum of trouble if you refrain from antagonizing the arrested woman, and avoid a show of emotion. If you *do* show emotion, you're on her territory, and you've given up your advantage. A woman has an arsenal of emotions she can change as fast as she can change her mind. You can't beat her at her own game. I can't stress that too much. Being diplomatic will help prevent friction.

"Now, with a woman there's always a question about handcuffs. Should? Or shouldn't? There's no S.O.P. about this. Your own judgment here. If you are in plain clothes—you've been on a stake-out, or responding in your own car to a call if you have a radio in your car, and if you don't you might want to think about getting one—handcuffs are an excellent identification. Casual observers may become aroused by seeing men pushing a woman into a car. If they see handcuffs, most people realize the men are engaged in official business.

"If there is a question in your mind about it, *any* obstreperous or unruly woman should be cuffed, for your own defense. Don't make the mistake of thinking just because it's a woman she can't hurt you. Even if she doesn't look that strong, she may have access to a weapon or a projectile. Once handcuffs are placed on an unruly woman, she *may* calm herself. She may promise to behave if her wrists are freed. (On the other hand, she may get hysterical.) If you use the handcuffs, once you have them on, it is not a good idea to remove them. Another thing, and this is important in terms of your own self-interest, women's hands are small and flexible and she may slip out of the cuffs if they are not properly adjusted. Handcuffs should be *double-locked*. Behind her back, with hands back to back.

"One more thing, *don't* touch her in any sensitive or questionable portion of her anatomy. If there's some reason to touch her, you think you have reason for a pat search, get a matron to do it. This should be self-explanatory.

"Remember that, in general, the less time you spend with a woman prisoner, the less chance there is for trouble."

I HAD ALWAYS taken domestics fairly lightly, perhaps because it was deeply interesting to me to arrive at someone's house at a moment of high emotion and to see people at their plainest, spitting and cursing and not caring who saw, but I don't recall ever feeling I was in any jeopardy. I learned eventually, though, that they were actually quite dangerous, and that I was rare in preferring a domestics call to one that required I search a dark building.

One night I answered a call with Chickie. It was about eleven. A woman had phoned the station asking for protection from her husband. Chickie knew the couple and—what I didn't know until afterward—he knew the man owned a gun, and he was concerned the husband might have gotten it out in the time between the call and our arrival.

When we got there, though, the couple had achieved some kind of peace. While Chickie stood in the living room and talked to the man—who seemed drunk and contrite—I watched the woman pack a small suitcase, make a phone call, and then collect her three children, who were wearing their pajamas, and take them out to the car. One of them didn't want to go. "Come on, honey, we're going for a ride in the car. Daddy's going to stay here. Lisa, honey, come *on!*" She took the child's hand and swept her out the door. I watched her load the car. She was a pretty, dark-haired woman, thin and tall and probably not very old, and she was on the point of collapse. She managed, though. When the kids were in and the doors were closed she came back to the house. She wanted the car keys.

"Where you going?" the man said.

"Never mind where I'm going. Away from you, that's all."

He took the keys from his pocket, gave them to her, and told Chickie he was going to bed. "You're all right?" Chickie said. "You want to call anybody?"

"No, no. Don't want to get anybody up this time of night. It's a goddam mess, though, isn't it? A goddam pretty mess."

We left and went to the Lighthouse. On the way Chickie was contemplative, and then he finally said, "It would be nice to sit down and take these people's minds apart, and see what makes them tick, but you just don't have the time. You've got to work fast." Joe was at the restaurant, fixing coffee and looking over the pie-rack. We all sat down together and I said something that re-called Chickie's remark about speed's being effective at a domestics.

"The thing about police work," Joe said, "is the faster you can do something, the better off you are. Sometimes just the fact that you *appear* to know what you're doing can distract people long enough to let you get your job done. Domestics are always tricky, though. I don't know what it is, but as soon as I get a call for a domestics, I get scared." (I remembered Paul had said, when I asked him what calls were the worst, "I feel more apprehensive an-swering a domestics call than I do for others. I calm down when I get there, but before, I get so nervous I could shit myself sometimes.") "I don't mean knee-shaking scared,"

Joe said now, "but something happens inside me—I'm worrying about what's going to happen, and who it is, and what type of problem it is. When I get there, I address the door the same way every time—bang, bang, bang, 'Who called'—but inside your stomach's turning a bit. You're going into a very emotional situation, where it's a family. You're in their environment. You don't know where they hide the knives, and they know where the gun is, if they have one, but you don't. A cop is always liable to get hurt when he's put at a disadvantage. And like Chickie said, you don't have time to get involved or listen to explanations. *Worst* thing you can do is take sides. You're always going to get two different stories anyway, and you can really get yourself in the poops by saying 'You're right and the old man's wrong,' or something like that.

"What you want to do is keep everyone in sight. Stay close to them. If someone has to leave the room—they have to go to the bathroom, make a phone call, get an address, anything at all—follow them, and don't turn your back."

"Charlie got a hatchet thrown at him one time," Chickie said. "He had just gone out the door and was walking back to the cruiser and *zingo*."

"By some lady, too," Joe said. "She missed. Hit a tree. Shook him up, though. Now, the best thing is to get a couple involved in a domestics out of the kitchen and into the living room. Kitchens aren't safe because that's where they have all the knives. Usually living rooms are safe unless you have some nut who keeps guns all over the place. There are people like that." I thought of a man Paul had introduced me to a few weeks before. Despite Wellfleet's being, by anyone's definition, a safe place to live, he had guard dogs, and a gun in every room. There were several in his living room, owing to its size.

"Important to remember it's going to make a difference who called you," Joe went on. "If it's one of the people involved—the wife says, 'I need help, my husband's drunk and he says he's going to beat me'—then they're going to expect you and they tend to be a little more under control when you arrive. Sometimes, a lot of times, in fact, you'll find that when one of the parties has called, the other has split before you get there."

"Especially if they've been drinking," Chickie said.

"If a neighbor or one of the kids calls, and they don't know you're coming, then you have a delicate matter. If they're not ready for you, and you *surprise* them, they're more likely to take offense at your presence. What you have to be concerned with is that this is another man's castle, and you don't want to upset the balance. You have to be cautious. You let them know that you're there on a complaint, and there's not going to be any more violence. You're not going to let them duke it out.

"One thing I do that has worked for me is I get the kids involved, you know, because that's often who calls in these cases, some kid, and he says 'My mommy and daddy are fighting and my mommy's bleeding'—something like that. What I say is 'Jesus, look at the kids, you're scaring them to death,' or 'What do you think the kids are thinking when they see this,' or 'That's a cute little kid,' anything to get their minds off the track of the problem, and then you'll usually find that the old man will take a walk. Before he leaves, though, and before *you* leave, you let them know that if you have to come back, someone's going to jail for the night. You have to be extremely careful, however. Sometimes you get a call back from the woman, and you arrest the man and you find she jumps all over you, 'You leave him alone, you son of a bitch,' or 'Where do you think you're going with him?' People are always worked up at these moments, and they don't always know their own minds."

Having grown up in Wellfleet, Chickie, Paul, the chief, the sergeant, Billy, and Charlie often knew the people to whose houses they were summoned. Sometimes they were friends, and every once in a while it might be a relative. Being familiar with the people, they might know, as Chickie had that evening, that the man owned guns, or that one of the people involved was often drunk, or had a tendency to be violent. I asked Chickie if the domestics we had just come from had been easier for him to handle because he knew the couple.

"With the people I know," he said, "when I get the call, right away, automatically, I know what the problem is. These people I didn't know that well, but if I can walk in somewhere and say 'Jimmy, what the hell is this for?' or something like that, that's an advantage. If I have to take someone to jail, it is *definitely* not an advantage to know them."

Later, I asked Paul the same question. "Sometimes have to psych myself more when I know the people," he said. "I have to think of all the potential hazards, and I have to put it in my mind that I can shoot if I have to—although I would never, ever want it to come to that—and I also have to put it in my mind that if I have to be a minister or reason with these people, I can do that, too. The worst thing is a lot of these people are older than I am, or they knew my parents, or they knew me when I was growing up, and they treat me like a goddam kid."

During the winter the outer Cape's bleakness and high unemployment rate and four-thirty sunsets make many people edgy and morose, and there is an abundance of domestics calls. Eventually I answered one on my own, on a four-to-midnight shift. I wasn't trying to be a hero; the sergeant had called in sick, and I was working alone that night.

I had with me in the cruiser Roland Dorval. He had just sold The Pub, and to bring in money and have something to do, he was learning to be a dispatcher for the police department. He had spent a few hours that night "on the board," supervised by Freda, and I was taking him home when Freda called and told me Merilee Russell had just phoned and said her estranged husband was banging on her front door. Merilee had a court restraining order forbidding his entering her house, and she wanted it enforced. (She probably knew from experience—but I didn't—that I had no authority to enforce it; that could be done only by the county sheriff.) Merilee's husband was practically twice my size, and I was worried about going there alone. Roland said, "I'll go there with you," and I felt relieved.

Merilee lived with her two children in a house by the pier. When Roland and I arrived, her husband was inside.

We could see him through a window. He was watching television. He was sitting on a bed, and he had his enormous back to us. I had heard from Chickie, who witnessed it, that one day at a construction site he had on his own shouldered into place a poured concrete wall. "You go ahead," Roland told me. "I'll wait here."

When I knocked, Merilee answered the door. She didn't say anything. I followed her down a hallway to a room at the end of it. "He's in there," she said.

The room was dark except for the light from the television. Her husband ignored us. He was watching a game show. "Hi, Frank," I said cheerfully. "What's the problem?" Somehow, I guess from Chickie's story, I felt I knew his name.

There was no response. "*You've* picked names and places," the TV announcer said. "For one thousand dollars, the capital of Colombia is Bogotá. True or false?"

"False," Frank said.

"You know you can't stay here, Frank," I said. Merilee nodded. She held up the order of conditions and waved it, like a little flag. It was a ratty-looking piece of paper and I had a feeling it had been repeatedly invoked in moments like this.

"Come on, Frank," I said, "you have to leave."

"I'm sorry," the announcer said, "it's true. But for a quick hundred dollars and our thanks for playing: who painted 'Whistler's Mother'?"

"Who painted Whistler's mother?" Frank said. "That's a low one. Who? His father?"

"That's right," said the announcer, "Whistler."

"Whistler?" Frank said. "That's the goddamdest one. Who painted Whistler's mother."

"Really, Frank, I mean it. I can't leave until you do."

Frank gave me a look, as much as to say he was trying to watch TV and I was distracting him.

I said, "Listen, Frank, I know you don't want to go, but you have to. Really.

"Frank, if it was up to me, you could stay. I can see all you want to do is watch television and you're sitting here quietly and not disturbing anyone, but you can't do it here. All right, Frank? Okay? Frank?"

"His name's David," Merilee said. "Well, if you'd asked I'd have told you, so quit staring at me like that. Frank's his brother."

"All right, I'm leaving, I'm leaving," David said. "Too much noise around here, anyway. But I'll be back. I haven't got nowheres else to sleep tonight and I'm not going to sleep in the car again."

On the way out he said, "Won't do you any good, Merilee, to lock up the door."

"Just you try," she said, the sweet thing, unfolding the paper again and waving it at him.

13.

Chickie Berrio

"I WAS WORKING concrete construction—I'd had my own business for about four years—and it got to the point finally where I was working only about ten hours a week because of the winter weather, and making about sixty bucks a week, and my bills were over a hundred bucks a week, and you just can't make it. One guy quit the force and there was an application out. Being a cop was a steady job, but it was the farthest thing from my mind.

"I came in to work and my first arrest was a guy named John Smith. I thought he was lying to me. He kept insisting his name was John Smith, and I told him mine was Hiawatha and threw him in the back of the cruiser."

Chickie's real name is Charles, and he and Charlie Valli grew up as neighbors in big houses on Commercial Street. Charlie remembers that Chickie used to call himself Charles C. Berrio. One afternoon when they were playing, Charlie asked Chickie what the C stood for. Chickie's mother, hanging out wash nearby, replied, "Chowderhead."

"Berrio is a French-Indian name from the Micmac Indians in Nova Scotia," Chickie once said. "There are six of us altogether in our family—I've got three brothers and two sisters. There are Berrios all over the Cape and I guess I'm related to most of them, one way or another. After I graduated from Nauset High, in 1965, I went into the service and stayed there until 1969, November. Served a tour in Nam. Worked the flight deck on a carrier landing planes and sending them off. During the day we were about eight miles off the coast and at night about three. When it got dark you could see the flashes on shore from the fighting. I didn't see any combat, but we had pilots on board who did. Lieutenant Carpenter, the pilot the North Vietnamese captured and paraded up and down, was on our ship. We didn't quite get to him in time with the helicopters. I ended up with five medals, the ones you usually get when you go into a combat zone—the American Defense, Vietnam Campaign, Vietnam Service, the Presidential Unit Citation, and the Good Conduct Brought them home and bought a cup of coffee with them.

"I liked the Navy. Got to travel. My favorite places were Japan, Greece, and Spain especially. I didn't like Italy, I wouldn't go back there. Then there was that place in South America I went to, Rio de Janeiro, that was nice. Brazil. Being a cop is not that different, I guess, from the Navy.

Shore patrol is something like police work, going into bars and breaking up fights, bringing people in. I had no idea how bad police work could get, though. I never *dreamed* of midnight-to-eight. I didn't foresee working every holiday and not having a chance to be with the kids— when everyone else is home carving their turkey dinner or their Christmas supper, you're out there riding around. My wife gets crank calls, because of the job. They know when I'm working, and they call when I'm not home. Just harassment. She broke her ankle jumping out of bed in the middle of the night once to answer one. Also, you're working all the time with people hooting and hollering at you. You start to characterize people. You can't help it. Some guy might not be nice and friendly and you call him a bum. Then after dealing with assholes all day or night, you're supposed to come home and be calm and joyful. It sounds good textbookwise, but it doesn't work. Also, I didn't foresee lack of friends. I know before I was on the force, we used to have company every night, and now we have company maybe once a week, or once a month. Also, you can't act like yourself. You have to go out of town to blow off steam. Most people forget that we're human. The public expects you to be a superhuman citizen. They don't expect or allow you to go out and kick up your heels like an animal occasionally. Working this type of job, and these hours, you have got to blow off steam sometimes. Otherwise they'd be committing us all."

14.

ALTHOUGH WELLFLEET IS a small town and round-the-clock protection might not really seem necessary, the Wellfleet police supply it. Every once in a while, over the winter, someone drinks too much and gets into his car at four in the morning and drives off and disappears into the woods and the police find him before he freezes, or someone smoking in bed falls asleep and starts a fire and the policeman patrolling happens to see it and alerts the fire department, and it justifies all the times that you ride around between midnight and dawn and nothing happens.

I worked midnights two or three, if not five, nights a week for seven and a half months. Beginning on Labor Day, when my Main Street tour was finished, I worked Saturday and Sunday during the day from eight until four. Sunday night I came back a little before midnight and worked until Monday morning. I worked midnight-to-eight again Tuesday, and Wednesday I worked four-to-midnight. In January I began working midnight-to-eight on Wednesday, too. In March and for part of April I worked midnights five nights a week. It was very depressing. I never seemed able to get enough sleep. As a result, I always seemed to have a cold.

I don't think anyone liked midnights. Whenever Joe Hogan got them, his wife used to call the chief and complain that it was impossible to raise a family and operate a household with the husband out all night and asleep all day.

"Midnight-to-eight just plays havoc with everything," said Joe. "Your system's shot to shit, there's no family life any more, you're coming home at eight in the morning, the phone's ringing and the television's on, the kid's are getting up, you're hollering at them to be quiet, it's normal for them to be up. You might as well go off on an island, you get so mean."

I tried a variety of sleeping schedules. I would go to bed when I got home in the morning and sleep all day; or get up at noon, then sleep again from eight until eleven; or stay awake all day and sleep from four until eleven and have breakfast at midnight; or sleep from noon until eight; or simply stay up until I felt tired and then sleep as long as I could; or take naps as I needed them; but none of these variations worked. It was always a different time of day for me. When I was asleep, everyone else was awake and when I was up and around, the town was dark and empty and quiet. It was impossible to make the simplest kind of plans. I couldn't, say, have dinner with anyone because if I was not asleep in the evening, I had no appetite, since it was not my hour of the day for a meal. When I did get out during daylight and see people I was so eager to have it mean something that I put them off. A woman I knew then told me later that she used to cross the street to avoid me during that period.

By the terms of the federal grant that made the funds available for my position, I did not have sick days, or vacation time, nor was I compensated for overtime, except that I could accumulate it toward days off. By February I had in my account a week's worth of court appearances and extra details, and just before I was to spend it the sergeant called me into his office. He wanted me to work a six-day week, filling in an extra night for Sherman, who was taking a day off, and then I could leave for my vacation a day early. The extra day was another midnight, which would make four that week. I didn't want to, I was sick of midnights, but I felt I should. It seemed small to complain. I said I would do it. The sergeant told me that when I came back, after my week off, I would be on a four-to-midnight schedule. I knew I had earned it—by that time I had worked many more midnights than anyone else—but I hadn't expected it and was grateful. I even felt sentimental when I thought of my last midnight and the things I would do to enjoy it.

When I came back to town a week later and went to the station at eight to work my regular Saturday shift and looked at the new schedule to be effective in a few days, found the sergeant had given me midnights five nights a week, with Sundays and Mondays off. I decided to quit and then thought it over and decided to talk first to the sergeant. I was sure he would change the schedule when I reminded him of his promise. If he didn't, then I'd quit. I would wait until 11:59 of the first night I was supposed to work to throw my badge and my gun on the desk in front of him.

I called the sergeant from the station. I knew he had worked until early that morning, and had probably been in bed only a few hours, but I thought it was fair that I woke him up, considering how many hours of my sleep he had ruined. With each ring of the phone, though, I felt less confident. I thought of a department meeting, one of the first I'd been to, at which Charlie Valli had complained of having had more midnights than anyone else. He said it was an awful strain on his family and on the trucking and hauling business he operated as a one-man endeavor, and he asked for relief. The slightly amused, even mocking tone of the chief's reply suggested that complaints about the vicissitudes of the work were signs of a weakness unworthy of a police officer. When the new schedule appeared several days later, Charlie had midnights from June to September.

The sergeant answered on the seventh ring. I had never called him at home before, but he didn't sound surprised to hear from me. He said we could meet at his house in an hour and hung up. Besides the regular duties of the shift, I had, as I did every Saturday and Sunday, one hundred vacant summer houses to check—I was responsible each month for visiting eight hundred of the town's twelve hundred cottages—and that would take the better part of the day, but I put off doing anything except reading the paper and drinking coffee until the sergeant and I talked.

As it happened, I didn't see the sergeant until that afternoon. He called the station and changed the time. We sat in his living room. He was watching a baseball game on television and half-listening to me. "I didn't say anything, Gary, over the summer, when I walked Main Street four hours a night, and my feet hurt, and I missed all the damn calls while the specials rode in the cruiser; I haven't complained about doing thousands of cottage checks while the others between them do several hundred; nor did I complain about babysitting *The Mischief*, though it was one of the worst nights of my life; I don't complain when you call me half an hour before I'm to be at work and say someone's sick and you're moving the midnight man to cover for him, and I have to work midnight; but this is it. You said I was going to have a decent schedule, for once."

The most considered response I got from him, delivered with his eyes on the game and from the side of his mouth, was, "I don't have to take this shit, you know." Finally he said, "And you don't either. Why don't you just quit if you don't like it?"

Finally, during a commercial, he said that the decision to assign me midnights had not been his, but the chief's. He said it would be only for a while. I suspected he had no idea how long it would be for, since it was the chief's decision, but I also saw that he felt bad about it.

After I had worked midnight-to-eights for three weeks, Hogan volunteered to take my place. The sergeant wanted me to think it was a handsome gesture on Hogan's part, but I knew better because I had talked to Joe; he simply wanted to get his midnights out of the way before the summer, which was the worst time to have them. Then, instead of changing monthly, the schedule was in effect for the season, and the heat made it difficult to sleep during the day.

15.

ASIDE FROM ESCORTING the school bus in the morning, and making sure no one passed it when it was stopped to take on children, all that was asked of the midnight man was that he check the doors of the town's businesses. To do this properly took an hour and a half. One rode through town and up and down Route 6, stopping in any order at each of the banks, shops, gas stations, and restaurants, inspecting the doors and windows, and then recording the time of the check. The idea was that if there had been a break-in the cop would discover it, or if the owner found it in the morning one could check back to the list and say the break must have happened between two, when the officer had found the building secure, and the time the owner had arrived. I never saw this information be remotely helpful as a clue.

One of my first nights doing the checks, I rode with Billy, who said he never did them twice in the same order on the theory that then no one could tell when or where he might turn up. I didn't like doing door checks—it was like having a paper route: getting in and out of the car, driving twenty feet or a hundred yards and doing it again, for an hour and a half—and I just tried to get them over as quickly as I could. I would start in the south and work north in order, or in the north and go south.

It didn't take me more than a couple of weeks to learn to estimate the times between stops and to be able then to fill out the time sheet without having to check the places thoroughly, or even sometimes to go there. By changing the order each night, I could always make it look like I went a different route.

The worst thing about door checks, though, was that every once in a while you would find a door open, and then you'd have to go inside. There were certain places I expected to find doors unlocked—Town Hall, for instance, was open so regularly that when Hogan found it secure one night he called in a "suspicious incident: Town Hall doors locked." I was in and out of Town Hall practically every midnight; I knew where the light switches were, and it was no problem. There was one building in town, however, that made me especially nervous, even though I had always found it locked. It had picture windows across the front and a glass door. In the dark, with the benefit of back-lighting from a nearby street lamp, the windows reflected my approach and were impossible to see through, except with my nose pressed to them. At times, walking up to the door and eyeing my reflection growing in the window before me, I felt sick at the possibility of someone's being inside and at the target I presented. One night I turned the handle of the door, and for the first time, it gave. I was alone, and it was about three o'clock. I shouted, dropped my flashlight, and tore off for the cruiser, reaching it after ten strides and breathing out of all proportion to the distance. I turned on the headlights and the spotlight and pointed the car at the windows, to light up the inside of the building, and drove slowly toward it, stopping when the distance between it and me was about fifteen feet. The parking lot was at a slight tilt to the foundation, though, and most of what my headlights showed was a section of the ceiling or the upper part of the back wall. The light cast shadows through the room, and I watched them for movement. Everything stayed still, still, still. I got a second flashlight and started again for the door. On the way the cruiser passed me: I had left it in gear. I dove in the driver's side window and jammed the shift lever to park. The car stopped two feet shy of the glass. I backed it up, out of the parking lot, onto the road and then across it, into another parking lot, and sat for some time, five minutes at least, looking at the half-open door and trying to calm myself enough to plan another approach. I was really shaken up. I tried to place myself in the mind of the person inside the building—if indeed there was one—and thought, *If I had broken into a building and it was dark, and I saw a cop approach by himself, no one else around, scream when he found the door open, drop his flashlight, run, and then nearly send a car through the plate-glass windows, would I try to escape because I thought he was overstimulated and might shoot me if I scared him? Or would I stay, thinking that he was incompetent and it would be nothing to overpower him?*

I found I couldn't answer the question. I considered a tactic of the chief's, which I had never used before, but I thought might work. He had come on it spontaneously when he was a patrolman, and he and his partner, Sandy Kmiec, responded to an alarm at the medical center.

"The guy had left a window open. Kmiec went in it," he told me, "and I went in after him. He's being quiet, but I was yelling and whooping it up, kicking in doors, saying, 'C'mon out, you son of a bitch, we're going to blow you away if you so much as got a gun with you,' you know, to get the psychological edge."

I didn't feel I could do that without a partner. I walked up to the door. Using the jamb as cover, I leaned my head into the dark room and took a deep breath. "I'm giving you ten seconds to be out here with your hands on your head," I said, "or I'm sending the dogs in."

I went back to the car, got the shotgun, looked around, and found no one there and nothing disturbed. On the way out I shut the door, picked up my flashlight, and bolted again.

IN WINTER, AS midnight-to-eight diversions, I learned, from Joe and Paul, to play spotlight tag—one cruiser hid and one was it, and you were tagged when the other found you and shone his light on you; to race nearly the length of the snow-covered lot at Newcomb Hollow, then lock your brakes, turn the wheel to one side, and spin the car in circles; to wait, when called, at the parking lot at Cumberland Farms, for Clem Silva, the Provincetown ambulance driver, who, returning from night runs to the hospital in Hyannis, would stop at the doughnut store there and fill the back of the ambulance with the day's expired doughnuts—which they gave him free, and which he then distributed among the police departments at Wellfleet, Truro, and Provincetown. Another diversion was to extinguish the streetlights in the town center by shining the spotlight on the light-sensing devices on top of them, and I once got almost all of them off in a circle from Main Street, to Bank Street, to Commercial Street, to Holbrook Avenue, and back to Main Street, twenty-eight lights, one and two tenths miles and nearly an hour's work. Or during certain hours I could drive the length of the highway from one end of town to the other, over seven miles, on the wrong side of the road, and not meet anyone. The police radio was occasionally diverting. On it I heard the K-9 dogs in Barnstable howling and sometimes the policemen howling with them. I heard train sounds, heavy breathing, sirens, and the patrolmen in Provincetown, who, when they got excited, spoke in Portuguese. One night Joe heard this exchange from Barnstable:

Dispatcher: Uh, EZ7, you want to check a report of a car on its roof on Route 137.

EZ7: Yeah, would that be an accident or what?

Dispatcher. Unless he *drives* it that way it is.

In Washington Joe once spent a midnight-to-eight in the company of a number of other officers making snowmen with huge sexual organs on the grounds of the Veterans Hospital. When they were done, they went and filled coffee cups with water and poured them over the snowmen's genitals to set them in ice. Joe also knew a policeman there who was about to retire and was troubled over never having fired his gun in the line of duty. It preyed on his mind until finally he drove out to the zoo one midnight and shot some deer.

To pass the time, I also used to listen to the late-night talk shows on the radio and to the interviews featuring people who were important in Providence or Boston or New Bedford or Fall River; and to the call-in shows with local radio personalities who discussed whatever was on people's minds: sports, taxes, show business, politics, drugs, and God. I listened often to a station from somewhere in the South that I knew about from Charlie and that we could only pick up after midnight. They played country music, and for an hour or so each night they played country comedy records. They had two. One had on it a few skits by Tennessee Ernie Ford, which involved his having arguments, in various settings (one, I remember, took place on a boat), with a woman partner named Blanche. The other record was by a man who specialized in reproducing sound effects, without props, and had worked them into his routine. My favorite station was in Rochester, New York. It had a jazz program every weeknight from midnight to five. The disc jockey strung together for an hour at a time records by McCoy Tyner, and John Coltrane, and Miles Davis, and Coleman Hawkins, and Sonny Rollins, and Pharoah Sanders, and a number of other people whose music I liked. When I put aside my feeling that I didn't want to be out there in the first place and concentrated instead on the huge clear sky above me, and the silence, or the music, and the feeling of having lots of time on my hands, I wasn't at all unhappy.

Working midnights, I shared people's secrets. I knew their arrangements. I knew, for instance, who waited until her husband was away fishing and then brought her boyfriend home, or met him at the beach. I certainly learned who stayed longest at the bars, and whom I would regularly find stumbling home in the cold, and what time I would find him, and at what place, and where to take him, and what to make, from practice, of his mumbling to me as I drove him home. (I knew also that he would never recognize me the next day when he was sobered up.) I used to drive every night past the house of a man I knew slightly and it caught my attention that the light in the bedroom he shared with his wife was always on, no matter what the hour. They both worked during the day, and I couldn't understand how they managed when they stayed up all night—or why they did. Finally I asked him and he said, "My wife can't sleep with the light off." There was a house by itself at the bay, in which lived an old man and his wife and his sister. Because they couldn't sleep well at night, they used to sit up and sew. Their house had big glass windows, and you could see it from a distance. It was eerie to come along the shore in the middle of the night, when the woods all around them were dark, and look in on the three of them, sewing.

Privacy was the advantage of midnights. Doing door checks, I often stopped at Mooney's Fuel and Grain, which occupied a long, faintly eastward-leaning warehouse on Duck Creek. I thought Mooney's building must once have had something to do with the fishing industry, because I knew that in the nineteenth century there were wharves in Duck Creek and the building looked large enough to have been the kind where fishermen unloaded their catches, or where boats were repaired; but actually it was built as a shoe factory when Cape labor was cheap, and reasonable shipping costs made that a lucrative site. The building had eleven small and large doors spaced at irregular intervals on its six sides (on the east side an indentation added two walls), and I don't know how big it was except that I counted one night that it took me one hundred and thirty-seven steps to circle it and shake each door.

In the middle of the night there was no breeze or motion on the water and no sound. It was totally calm and strange. A stilled Duck Creek became an opaque mirror, and looking east across it from Mooney's, one saw the town and its precise reflection. Rising above the trees, the steeple of the Methodist church and the tower of the Masonic temple in the center were the prominent details of this nightscape. Across the creek there were thirty-two lights; sixteen reflected in the water and their sixteen sources above them (the lights over the street, a few porch lights, and the rest from the police station, directly across the way). The third landmark, Uncle Tim's bridge, a footpath that crossed Duck Creek and connected the town proper to Cannon Hill, bisected the right half. I found a photograph of exactly this scene, taken in daylight and titled "The Village of Wellfleet," in a booklet advertising the opening of the Chequesset Inn in 1902.

I never found any doors open at Mooney's, and I don't think I would have gone in if I had. Not alone, anyway. It was too big and had too many hiding places. And since it was partly a feed and grain store, there must have been some mice, and a cat, perhaps, to chase the mice, and any noise, however slight, such as they might make would have been sinister in the dark.

The Mooneys parked their three six-wheeled heating oil delivery trucks on the south side of the building. Some nights I climbed to the roof of the first truck, stepped across the other two to the top of a ten-foot hill of peat moss bundles, and from that height made my way easily into the branches of a nearby locust tree, where I sat peacefully surveying the cove. Other nights I went straight to the abandoned hull stranded by the tide at the edge of the marsh and pretended to be captaining a launch.

Paul, who was more ambitious than I was, used to keep busy on midnights by arresting drunk drivers. During the winter I got the idea that I could work my way off midnights by making a lot of arrests, so I began to go after drunks too. They were easy to get—there were so many of them that I have never felt safe on the roads after dark since. It had no effect on my schedule, but for a while I led the department in arrests.

There were many kinds of drunks. Some drove at moderate speeds, carefully and with concentration, except on the wrong side of the road. Some drove at a crawl, although I believe they thought they were actually going fast. Others drove hell for leather, and all over the place. One man I saw was stopped, but believed himself to be speeding down the road; he was making engine noises through his lips. I once watched another man step out of a restaurant where he had been drinking and into his car, then start it up, and head off in reverse, all the time staring dead ahead, under the impression that he was traveling forward. He came to rest with a crash against another car, but he didn't know it; he continued to run the engine and spin his wheels in the gravel. I walked up and tapped on the window and asked for his license. He lifted his foot from the accelerator, applied the brake, and when he was satisfied he had brought the car to a proper stop, he put it into park. It took another man I stopped several minutes to find his license. He fished through his wallet and studied everything carefully, finally located it, and handed it over. He wore a broad grin. It was apparent he thought it had taken him only a few seconds. The card he gave me entitled him to a 10 percent discount at a car wash.

Some drunks were fastidiously polite, some were scared and meek, and some were belligerent. It had nothing to do with size or sex, or any other factor I could think of. There was no accounting for it.

Most people I stopped had gotten drunk in Provincetown, where there were several bars open in the winter. On their way south they came first through Truro, where Dennis Divine, who worked midnights while I did, was waiting for them. After he had caught one and was on his way with him to the jail, I could get the next one that came along. The hour to get them was between quarter to two and quarter to three, and I could nearly always count on getting one. Some nights I would let a few go by until I had one who was very drunk and certain to score high on the Breathalyzer—I didn't want a cheap arrest. One night I arrested a man, drove to Orleans with him, booked him and did my paperwork, and was back in Wellfleet an hour later and got another one.

One midnight when I was by myself I arrested a man who was bigger than Billy Brooks. His name was Rufus Gross, he was six-foot-seven, and I had no idea of his size when I pulled his car over. I had seen a pair of taillights moving slowly down the center of the highway. They lurched right, and several seconds later, when they moved into the other lane, I put on the blue lights and called in my stop. As I was talking to the dispatcher, Rufus got out of his car. "And I'll need a backup," I said. (I was working with the sergeant, who was on until two, but he was out of his car and didn't have a radio and the dispatcher wasn't able to reach him until I was already on my way to the lock-up in Orleans.)

I requested the man's license and his registration, which he gave me, pointed out a line painted at the edge of the highway, and asked him to walk it for me. He turned to look at it and started off, taking very small steps, embellishing rather than strictly pursuing the line. He turned and came back. I told him to close his eyes, extend his arms to the sides, and with them extended, to try to bring his index fingers together in front of his face. He was obviously drunk, and I was going to arrest him, but I couldn't figure out how to get him in the cruiser. He tried several times to touch his fingers and he couldn't do it but he liked trying, so he kept at it. I reflected on a story I had heard from the chief about another small Wellfleet patrolman who, working alone one night, had also pulled over a man larger than he. The man was drunk and agreeable until the officer mentioned arrest and brought out his handcuffs. The man then folded his arms across his chest and said, "It's going to take a lot more than you to get those things on me." He got back in his car and drove off, and the officer had to organize some troops to go to the man's house and pick him up.

"Okay, that's enough right now," I said. "Would you come and have a seat in my cruiser, Mr. Gross? I'd like to ask you just a few more questions."

He walked toward the front seat, but I rushed ahead of him and held open the back door. When he had folded himself into that small space I slammed the door. "Mr. Gross," I said, "you're under arrest for operating under the influence of alcohol." He tried the door.

On the way to Orleans I asked him if this was the first time he had ever been arrested. He said no, there had been one other time.

"What was that for?"

"Turning in an assassin of the president of the United States," he said.

One brings prisoners to the jail at the Orleans police station through garage doors that are electronically controlled by the dispatcher. You call when you arrive, and they open the doors and close them behind you. The booking officer comes down a hallway from the central part of the station and meets you at a heavy metal door that he opens from his side. Once in the garage, I stepped out of the car and waited a moment to give the booking officer time to get started before I let Rufus out. I led him to the door and stood with him. Opening the door, the booking officer met my eyes and the middle of Rufus' chest and looked up, and then immediately down to see if I had cuffed his hands.

In the station I had my first opportunity to study Rufus. He was dressed in old clothes and a shabby coat that reached his waist. His pants bagged around the tops of a pair of Wellingtons that were exceptionally large. He had a gaunt face, bad teeth, a hawk nose, a thin beard in the hollows of his cheeks, and he stooped.

For the booking officer, he spoke in something that sounded at first like Latin, and then more and more like double-talk. He had a few moments when he talked intelligibly, and during one of these he repeated the story of his arrest for turning in a presidential assassin. This was in response to the booking officer's asking if he had a prior record, and at the unexpected reply the officer began chewing his lower lip. He left the Previous Arrest space on the form blank.

When Rufus had been booked and had emptied his pockets of a comb, some change, and a wallet, the three of us, the booking officer in the lead and Rufus in the middle, walked down the hall. Rufus blew into the Breathalyzer's mouthpiece and waited for the machine to reply, and I did my paperwork. I saw him being led to a small cell in which were a cot, a blanket, a sink, and a toilet. They were small to begin with, and ridiculous for someone the size of Rufus. According to the Breathalyzer he was very drunk, and when I left he was curled up on the cot, preparing to sleep it off.

At ten, after handling Rufus' arraignment, Billy called. "That guy you arrested last night went nuts," he said. "He tore up the Orleans police station."

"What do you mean?"

"Louise, the lady who dispatches, said she heard a noise, like a banging, in the middle of the night, and she looks on the video cellblock monitor they have there, and sees this guy standing with the toilet raised up over his head. He just pulled the goddam toilet out of the wall—the thing's bolted into the pipes, and he puts his hands on it and pulls it out—*rips the frigging thing right out of the wall! Lifts* it over his head and *smashes* it on the floor."

"You're kidding. This is a joke. He was going to sleep when I left."

"Well, he woke up. You should see the photographs. Then he drops his pants and takes a dump on the floor,' great big pile, like a horse. I don't know if he was scared or what. *Louise* was scared he was going to bend the bars and get out, but I guess he just walked around awhile and went back to sleep. The janitor's bullshit about having to clean up the floor. When they asked him why he did it he said there wasn't any toilet paper. Jesus. They didn't even want to get him out this morning for court. They thought he might still be crazy."

The chief was amazed I had made the arrest without help.

While Rufus was being arraigned, the Orleans police checked his story about the presidential assassin. They found nothing to back it up, but they did learn that a year or so before, Rufus, carrying a gun, had broken into a radio station somewhere in Massachusetts and held the staff at bay, and seventy-five policemen had taken an hour to subdue him. He had been charged with five counts of assault with a deadly weapon and was convicted and placed on probation.

Rufus came to trial several weeks later. I saw him at the courthouse and he didn't recognize me as the one who had arrested him. "You know that cop who brought me in," he said, "I don't have any complaint, it was a good arrest, fair enough, but he was a little guy. I could have dented his head on the roof."

On the witness stand, which is elevated, Rufus looked unnaturally tall and gaunt. I waited for the question about the toilet, and when it came I was surprised at his reply. To answer "Would you please tell the court, Mr. Gross, what happened to the toilet in your cell?" Rufus pinched the thumb and index finger of his right hand nearly together and brought them close to his eyes, and moving them away slowly to trace a line as he spoke, said, "A little energized particle broke off a star in a galaxy someplace far away and shot down and came through the open window, and when it hit the toilet, *BOOM*"—he jerked his arm up and raised his eyebrows—"the whole thing blew up. I could have been killed." No one mentioned that he had afterward moved his bowels on the floor, but the judge saw the pictures.

The judge declared Rufus guilty of "drunk driving" and assessed him $43.75 in fines plus $115 to repair the toilet. Rufus did not appear disturbed by the verdict. He paid his fine quietly and left.

WHEN THE WORK schedules changed, and I saw that month after month, arrests or no arrests, I kept getting midnights, I gave up and started sleeping. The word for falling asleep on your shift was *cooping*, and I have no idea what it was derived from. According to Hogan, in Washington, D.C., the word for cooping is *hoodling*. I had fallen asleep a few times during the summer, but I hadn't meant to. Once, on a drowsy, rainy night, I fell asleep on the porch of the Lighthouse and the sergeant caught me and bawled me out, which annoyed me, because sleeping on the job wasn't anything I hadn't seen him do. It was hard to stay awake late at night as a passenger and I had fallen asleep a couple of times when I was riding in the cruiser with Hogan. The first time he waited until my eyes were closed and my head slumped forward and then he screamed. The second time the window on my side happened to be open and he drove me slowly past a lawn sprinkler.

I had trouble falling asleep when I was alone in the police car. The others, when they slept, which was not often, liked to find a place by the highway and then park, on the theory that if anything happened to them they would be found. (As a precaution, one of them used to lay his gun across his lap.) I slept in the woods, or at the beach, because I was more worried that I would be caught than that something might happen to me. The problem was that I used to have hallucinations and I would hear things. I would stir for a moment in my sleep and half-open my eyes and then jump up alert, because I thought the horizon was glowing with the headlights of an approaching car. On other occasions, though I was deep in the woods, and it was impossible, I would hear a car passing and start awake. Or I would dream and imagine my own car was moving and out of control and about to crash and I would wake up and frantically search the darkness outside for a static object to compare myself to. It never occurred to me to check the speedometer.

I had enough trouble with it that I gave up sleeping outside and tried to nap in the station. I got some chairs from the evidence closet tagged "Case #742234," set them up in a second closet, closed the door so it was dark, and then stretched out between them. I put a file folder on the floor next to me so that in case someone came in the station I could step from the closet, apparently studying records. I couldn't sleep in the closet, either, because I didn't trust the dispatcher not to report me to the rest of the department. I went back to the road and accustomed myself to the hallucinations.

16.

Charlie Valli

I FELT MORE at ease with Charlie than anyone else. All the other men interested me as people, and I gained from their company, but I had no experience in common with any of them. Charlie and I shared an affection for the woods, and to me that made a bond. Charlie's knowledge of the woods was comprehensive.

Charlie stood above six feet. He had heavily muscled arms and sloping shoulders that stretched the seams of his police shirt and caused them to ride up under his arms, even though police shirts are cut to accommodate normally large-shouldered men. He was then in his early thirties, but his face was deeply lined. It made him appear weary, even when he was rested. His hair was blond and receding slightly. He wore it cropped on the sides and a little longer on top, and parted it precisely. He had a cowlick he disciplined with a tonic that left his hair stiff. Most of the time his hair looked like that of a child just returned from the barber. That and the asperity of his face made a startling combination, like an old man wearing a wig. The flexible metal band of his watch stretched over his wrist, leaving small gaps between the links. I could have produced the same effect by wearing the band on my arm, near the elbow.

When Billy Brooks was promoted to prosecutor and to the day shift, Charlie replaced him on midnight-to-eights. Whereas Billy had been in the habit of sleeping after work in the mornings, Charlie breakfasted with his family, changed his clothes, hid his gun, and began the heavy physical work of the trucking and hauling business he operated by himself. As if that weren't enough, he was also a member of the volunteer fire department and the rescue squad. He quit work around four o'clock, and by four-thirty he was in bed. How well he slept depended on how quiet the kids were and whether or not a call from the fire department or the rescue squad interrupted him. He rose around eleven, his wife and children were asleep, and when he came back to work at midnight, he seldom looked rested.

He was able to keep himself awake by discipline. He never drank coffee, or took any medicine, for that matter. When he felt tired—and he didn't consider himself so unless he had fallen asleep and run off the road—he came to the station and did paperwork, or read law, or swept the place up.

Charlie had been on the police force intermittently since 1967, the same year he began his trucking business. At first he was a special and therefore considered part-time, though he worked a forty-hour week, dispatching two nights a week and riding in the cruiser for three. As the police force expanded, the need to employ specials year-round diminished, and Charlie's hours were reduced to where he did most of his work in the summertime. In January 1975 he became full-time and was back to forty hours a week.

"I like the work a lot," he said one night. "But some things don't make sense to me. Right now I work on the police force, my wife stamps cans in the supermarket, and she makes more money than I do. I have to work mid-night-to-eights and swing shifts." Swing shifts mean working the other men's days off, so that you might in one week have two four-to-midnights, two midnight-to-eights, and an eight-to-four. "It's especially difficult because I have to work two jobs, which is not really the police force's fault, except that they don't pay me enough that I can work only one job. If I could work one job, then it wouldn't be so bad; I would have days off, and I could be sure to be around when the kids got home. Now I'm on a four-to-midnight shift. The kids get back from school, and I'm going out the door. My oldest boy doesn't get home until after I've left, so I never see him unless I have a chance to come home for supper."

Several years before I was a policeman, Charlie ran for selectman, against a woman, and lost. Subsequently he resigned his positions on the fire department and the police department. The selectmen control both, and he refused to work for a woman. When she resigned, because she was moving out of town, he returned. While I was a policeman another woman was running, and Charlie said that if she won, he would resign again. The woman was intelligent and qualified and I favored her election (she lost, narrowly) but I didn't enjoy being at odds with Charlie, whom I liked a great deal. One evening during the selectman's campaign I tried to talk him out of resigning. We were at his house.

"It's just an opinion based on the way I feel about life and people," he said. "I just don't believe that women should be leaders of men. I believe that man is the head, and as far as I'm concerned any woman who thinks she's equal to a man isn't worth her salt as a woman. And I won't have one signing my appointment, either. One does, and I'm gone. I don't believe in the Equal Rights Amendment, and I never will. My belief is taken straight from the Book of Genesis: woman will be a helpmate to the man and she won't be a leader. Course I'm outnumbered nowadays, but that's all right. It'll change. The problem is everyone is too interested in having too many freedoms. We weren't meant to have all this many freedoms. Somebody has to be a leader and somebody has to be a follower. In my house my wife and I are equals in everything we do together, in making decisions, and in raising the family. If she disciplines the kids I'll back her up, and vice versa. But if we have a disagreement, and we *can't* come to an agreement, my word is going to be the final word. If we had a disagreement and we were both equal, it wouldn't work.

The only solution would be to part. And then who suffers? We both suffer, the kids suffer, society in general suffers. So you get an awful fine line there and I think some of the old standards ought to be ready at hand."

One of his boys, as tow-headed as Charlie must have been at that age, came in and asked his father a question about his homework. Charlie supplied the answer and then he turned back to me. "The other day the youngest one comes home saying that he came from fish. He says, 'Now I don't believe that, Dad, and I know you don't believe it, but that's what they're teaching me in school.' So I said, 'They're getting into evolution, huh?' and he says, 'Yup.' 'Well, you get them to prove one of those evolutionary theories,' I said. And they can't do it. Every one of them they'll attach the word theory to, and if you look up the definition of *theory*, you'll find it doesn't mean fact. As far as I'm concerned, our faith has something that's tried and true. Everything you check back on in the Bible is provable. So that's the way I base my life and it gets me along. It's a great life if you don't weaken."

WHEN HE WAS growing up he used to ride his bicycle after school along the sand roads that wind in and out among the ponds. "I always liked going in the woods," he once told me. "It's quiet. No crowds. As a kid I spent a lot of time alone there. When I got a car I spent more time on the dirt roads than I did on the highway." He hunted there as well but eventually gave it up. "I was brought up in a family where there was a lot of hunting going on and

I began when I was young. I was a good shot and I could kill the animals quick. One time, though, I went duckhunting with my brother. We were walking along the marsh by the Herring River and two ducks flew over and landed behind us and I said, 'Well, I'm going to get those two ducks.' He went on to get his ducks and when I got back to the far end of the marsh the two ducks started to the air and bam, bam, I shot them, and they both went down. I went over and picked up the first one, fine, he was dead, and I go over to the other duck. He was looking at me. When it got to a confrontation like that I just couldn't kill him. I guess since I got older I got softer about killing. If I can just go out and kill them, it doesn't bother me. But if they suffer, that bothers me.

"I didn't hunt again for a while. Then one day I went out after pheasant. They were all over the place, they had just been stocked, and I guess it must have been opening day of the season, because there was a bunch of hunters, too. You couldn't shoot in any direction for the crowds. Well, I was walking across a field and I turned around and looked over my shoulder and there was a hunter behind me, at the far end of the field, and right in between us a pheasant jumped up. I said, 'Hey, look at that,' knowing full well he couldn't shoot at it. So he shot at it. The pellets were running all around my feet. I said, 'That's it.' Went home and put my gun away. Now I just like to go in the woods and sit and look."

He was fond of driving me down one of the number of sand roads I knew and, when he sensed I had already made up my mind about where he was headed, making a turn here or there and ending me up completely lost. And then making another turn and showing me we were in practically the same place he had taken me to a few days before. We had only come at it from a different approach. He would laugh and laugh.

Although Charlie loved the woods, he was not in favor of the national park that preserved them.

"The park ruined everything. They gave a raw deal to a lot of people who live around here, including my own family. They took land by eminent domain, and gave five thousand dollars for a piece of property that fifteen years ago the people had been offered a hundred thousand dollars for. It just wasn't right. The turning point for me was going down to Dyer's Pond and seeing the fish floating belly-up in the soap suds from all the people taking baths. I remember when you used to be able to drink out of Dyer's Pond, and Duck Pond, and all them other ponds. You can't even swim in them nowadays in the summer for fear you'll catch something or the soap will smart your eyes. That was all brought on by the park. The minute it came in, boy, *zoom* went the crowds. Before that the town population might double or triple from the winter, but I don't know how many times it goes over now. I can't even leave my car at the beach on a day off. You can't get a space unless you get there at eight in the morning.

"I know what it is to live in a little town, and I know what it is to live in a place that's not quite a little town but that's not a city either. My heart has always been with the little town. It's to the point now where, if something should appear for me someplace else, I'd probably take it. Four years ago I would have said, 'Charlie Valli would never say that.' I used to go away and I couldn't wait to get back to Wellfleet. Now it's just plain too crowded. When I look through the windows at night I like to see the trees, the moon, the stars. And the storms. A friendly light is nice, but I like to see it a little farther away."

17.

ON MY THIRD night Paul took me to a rescue call for a man who had had a heart attack. When we arrived, Sherman was already there, kneeling and holding an oxygen mask in place above an old man who was stretched the length of a couch, with a blanket drawn from his feet to his chest. Behind Sherman a television set was on, but the sound was turned off. The man's face was blue and his jaw hung loose. His wife, a small, gray-haired woman, stood in the far corner of the room, by a bookshelf, twisting her apron in her hands. She had complete trust in Sherman and in the doctor who was on his way, and she was unaware that her husband was already dead, and that the doctor who was coming was the medical examiner to pronounce him so. "We were watching TV," she said, "like we always do after dinner—he likes to lie down and watch—and he fell asleep, which he will do sometimes. I was sitting next to him, in the green chair over there, doing a puzzle, and he made a sound like he was groaning, and then when I called him he wouldn't wake up. I couldn't wake him up. I don't know what's wrong."

A few men from the local rescue squad walked in. One of them, younger than I was, leaned toward me and said, "Tell Sherman it's a code ninety-nine."

"What?"

"Tell Sherman it's a code."

Later I learned this stood for cardiac arrest. I whispered it to Sherman, who said, "I know."

He held the oxygen mask several inches above the man's face, too high to be of any help, and in fact the oxygen was nearly turned off, but he understood what the woman was thinking and he held it there for her sake, and because it wasn't his business anyway to say the man was dead. The room had filled up with men from the rescue squad. I saw them open a passage at the door and the doctor, a large, forceful man, strode in. Everyone formed a circle around him and the couch, and the woman and I joined its edge.

"There's no need for oxygen," the doctor said. "This man's expired. It'ss obvious. Didn't anyone call the funeral home yet?"

The woman's composure gave way all at once. The circle dissolved. Sherman stood up. I went outside and across the lawn, beyond the police cars and the ambulances and the car belonging to the men of the rescue squad, and walked a small circuit to calm myself. When I went back in, the men from the funeral home had arrived and were preparing to take the body. The woman was on the phone and I heard her say, "Your father died tonight."

ONE MORNING AT dawn, deep in the woods, Paul found a car, and inside it a man who had asphyxiated himself by running a hose from his exhaust pipe through the window. Several days earlier the man's family had reported him missing. Paul knew him slightly and had seen him in that part of the woods before, and hearing he had disappeared, he went there to look for him.

I was called in to cover the town while Paul saw to the removal of the body. I gave the chief a ride into the woods. When we arrived, Paul was standing in a clearing, about fifty feet from the car, which had been driven as far as it would go up an abandoned and overgrown dirt road. The chief looked in the window and said, "Yup, he's dead," and returned to the cruiser. "I never had a passion for viewing dead bodies," he told us.

The medical examiner arrived then, and the chief went to talk to him. I stayed with Paul. "I waited until the light came up," he said. "I wasn't going to go in there in the dark. I saw the car and went up to talk to him, course he's dead, I knew it, I figured he was. I talked to him anyway. In case his spirit was still around."

ONE SPRING AFTERNOON when I came in to work, Lori, the daytime dispatcher, told me that Billy and Chickie had just left to handle a suicide call, and they had taken both cruisers. I asked her if she would give me a ride there—it was time for her to leave and the house was on her route home—but she said she wouldn't go near a house that had a dead body in it. Someone else took me, I forget now who, and left me in front of a cottage on a sandy lot near an inlet of the bay. I had been to the house the day before while doing cottage checks. The cruisers were parked in the driveway. The front door stood open. Inside an old man sat in a chair, with his hands folded in his lap. He stared across the bay and paid no attention to me, seemed not even to know I was there. I heard Billy and Chickie in the basement and went down the stairs. The cellar was damp and musty from being so close to the water and not having much light. Billy and Chickie were standing on either side of a man hanging by the neck from a rope attached to the pipes overhead. He had his back to sliding glass doors, which looked onto a broad, untroubled view of the marsh. His feet rested on the floor and his legs were bent at the knees because the pipes weren't high enough overhead to allow him to hang himself any other way. If he had stood up, he couldn't have managed it. His head, level with my shoulder, slumped forward and to the right. His expression was sad, as if he were still distressed. He had socks on, and they bagged at the tips. "Toes amputated," Chickie said. "Diabetic."

When I mentioned to Billy the coincidence of my having checked the house the day before, he said, "And you mean you didn't *see* him?" I had been in a hurry and instead of walking around the place and trying all the doors and windows, I had only left a slip at the front door. I was relieved when the medical examiner arrived and told us the man had been dead only a few hours.

Chickie wrote notes and made measurements for his report, the county investigating officer took pictures, and when Brian, the man from the funeral home, arrived, we cut the rope and lowered the body to the floor.

The knees stayed bent. The rope had bit and left a seam, and the neck had swelled to several times its normal girth. Brian poked at it and said, "I don't know how I'm ever going to get that down for an open casket."

He had brought a collapsible stretcher, with wheels and a body bag. We lifted the man into it. To fit him in Brian had to straighten the legs and one arm. He did it quickly, and the joints cracked.

On our way out we passed the man upstairs in the chair. He appeared not to have moved at all. "Guy's brother," Chickie said. "He was here the whole time. Deaf. Never heard a thing."

"How did you find him?"

"His wife called the station and asked us to deliver a message to him. They live somewhere up-Cape, Hyannis, I think, and they were finishing up building this house. They don't have a phone here yet. She wanted us to see if he was here, and have him give her a call."

I remembered that afternoon because it was the first hanging I had ever seen. Chickie remembered it because coming from bright sunlight into the darkness of the basement he had bumped into the man. "I dreamt about that guy for months," he said. "I used to see his face looking at me."

ON A FRIDAY night a few days before Christmas in a small cottage off one of the roads that lead to the bay, a young woman hanged herself. When found, she was still warm, and had the person who discovered her known how to perform resuscitation, it might have been possible to bring her back to life.

I saw her the next day at the funeral home. I was there as a witness to the autopsy. It was held in a small white room in the funeral home. There were seven of us altogether: Sherman and me, the county investigating officer, the funeral home director and his assistant, and the two medical examiners—one a local doctor, who was also here as a witness, and the other a doctor from up-Cape who would perform the operation. The body lay on a table in the center of a chamber on the first floor of the funeral home. We stood in a circle around it. A partially shaded window allowed the only natural light, and a small fan circulated the air. Joe had told me earlier that morning that the worst thing about an autopsy is the smell of the body, but I didn't notice any. The girl's head was supported by a block of hard rubber under her neck. The table tilted slightly toward her feet in order to drain fluids into a bucket hanging there. A hose attached to a deep stainless-steel sink provided suction.

The doctor laid out his tools, sets of shiny scalpels and a large pair of surgical shears. He donned rubber gloves and turned the body face down to check for any signs that death had occurred from something other than hanging.

The other side was crimson, because the blood had settled overnight. He found nothing suspicious, and turned the body over. Using a scalpel he traced a line from the base of the throat to the crotch. The borders of the incision bled slightly. He flayed the skin back, and cut the breastbone with the clippers. He drew a blood sample, with a vial, from inside the chest cavity. As the operation progressed he removed various organs and examined them. He cut and bagged sections of them and sent them to the police labs for analysis. What he discarded, the funeral home director placed in a small box, like a cat-litter box, on the floor. Each time he put something in, he covered it with a powder that looked like sawdust. Sherman recorded the time of every step.

The doctor was the only one who spoke. His remarks were macabre. He paused to describe a case he had recently handled that involved a man who had murdered his best friend and then covered the corpse with lime, under the impression that it would speed decomposition. "Well, you see, lime preserves," said the doctor, "and when the body was discovered a year later, it was easy to tell who it was, and how he had died, and to find the murderer." He paused, a scalpel in his right hand, and scratched the end of his nose with a gloved wrist. "Not at *all* what the killer had in mind."

When he removed the womb he said, "Let's see if we can't find any little strangers in here."

The final task was the removal of the brain. To accomplish this, the doctor had a small electric saw with a circular blade mounted flat on a handle that looked like a flashlight. It made a whirring noise. The doctor held it to his arm. "You'll notice it doesn't cut a smooth surface like skin," he said, "no matter where I place it." He touched it lightly and rhythmically to his arm. "Only bone."

With a scalpel he cut the skin along the girl's hairline. He put the blade down and peeled the face back on itself. Using the saw, he cut a line through the top of the skull from ear to ear, and then joined it across the forehead. The progress was slow. Bone fragments chipped loose, spun in the air, and fell to the floor. There was a dusty, smoky odor. When the cut was made and the portion of the skull removed, the doctor, using both hands, fished out the viscous mass. He examined it and removed a small section, and then like all the parts before it, it was placed in the box on the floor and covered with sawdust. The operation was over.

I walked outside to the cruiser, which I had left on Main Street. It was late Sunday morning. The churches were out. The street was empty and still and I got in the car and drove.

For weeks afterward, before falling asleep, or when my mind was clear of thought, images from that morning came back to me, and though they had not upset me at the time, because it had all been so clinical, they upset me later.

18.

Joe Hogan

I WOULD HAVE quit if it hadn't been for Joe Hogan. The hours of pleasure I had in his company sustained me when I felt miserable over the schedule I worked, or hated walking Main Street, or had been planted on some detail and left by the sergeant. Or was lonely.

Joe was born into a large family in Brockton, Massachusetts.

"I grew up in a veterans' project, and there were probably about two hundred kids there, so there was never a lack of something to do. We played hard, awful hard. We used to have a game—I wonder who the hell made this game up—you put a guy up against a wall. Snow, right? And everyone would get back about ten feet and make snowballs. And he's facing you. And here's the object of the game: to throw the snowball as hard as you can, and as *close* as you can, without hitting him. If you hit him, you're up there. That's the type of stuff we used to do. We were always getting screwed up, and beat up, and hurt, fighting and carrying on. I was a bastard, not criminalwise, but I had a good time. One time there were houses all along in rows, and they all had chimneys, and I decided I was going to put the fires out in the houses. I got up on the roof, and my brother Tommy handed me a pail of water, and I went down and threw it in the first chimney and ran back. I got three of them. People came out to see if it was raining. It was a clear night and all of a sudden this big splash comes down the chimney. I got yanked off the roof for that.

"My father played piano and music was important. I was dumb in school, very dumb, but enough to get by to graduate when I was supposed to. Played Little League, used to be a good army man when I was a kid, had a good time in the woods. Normal, I guess.

"Went into the service after high school, got out, joined the Metropolitan Police Force in Washington, D.C. That's where I hurt my back. I'd been there about five months when I got a call to assist another cruiser. When I got there I found two guys scuffling with a man they had pinned on the floor.

"One of the cops had his handcuffs out and was trying to cuff the guy on the wrist, and the guy wouldn't let him do it. What it was, was the guy was sick; he'd had a fit and they were trying to restrain him. I didn't know that at the time. I just figured the guy was under arrest. So when the guy's hand broke free I stepped on the wrist. I had my stick in my hand. When the guy's kid saw that he said, 'Don't you hit him, you bastard.' I wasn't going to hit him. I didn't even pay attention to the kid because I was bending down so I could take my foot away and grab his hand. The next goddam thing I know the kid latches onto my neck, and he grabs my hand with the stick with his other hand. We were only five feet from the door, and he had the momentum, so I went right back with him, out the door, onto the porch and down the steps. Missed all three steps of concrete. Landed flat on my back. *Boom*, he landed right on top of me. Woke up the next morning and couldn't move. If I'd had my wits about me I'd have put in a disability claim and got out of it with sixty-six and two thirds.

"Later I hurt it again. I got a call. I don't know what day it was, but it must have been a weekend because they only shoot each other on weekends. I'm by myself in the car and I hear 'Car One-three-four and One-two-seven, you have a report of a criss-cross shooting, two ambulances responding. First unit on the scene advise.' I pull up in front of the house. There's two guys laying on the lawn moaning and groaning, and there's a couple of women standing on the lawn shouting and hollering at each other. Meanwhile cars are going back and forth in the street, and there isn't anybody stopping to help. I get out of the cruiser and say, 'What's going on?'

"Now, I didn't know that these two had shot each other. I had got the word that it was a criss-cross shooting, which means that both of them had guns, but that's not the way it always happens. That's the way they might have wanted it to be. It could very well have been that one of those people standing there had shot both of them, that somebody they didn't know had shot them. Whatever. There were no guns at the scene. I went over to the women and I said, 'Who's got the guns?' 'We ain't got no muhfuckin' guns. Somebody came up and shot them muhfuckers.' I said, 'I want to know where the gun is. Who's got the goddam gun? Where is it?' 'There ain't no muhfuckin' gun.' I said, 'Jesus Christ, lady, where's the pistol? Who's got it? Has he got it on him?' 'I ain't got no gun,' she says. 'I heard two shots, I don't know what happened. Some muhfucker came up shot my husband dead.'

"So I bend down, and I'm talking to this guy on the ground, and he says, 'I'm all right,' and the other guy says, 'I'm all right.' They're both smoked anyway, been drinking. And then one of the wives starts it. 'It was that muhfucker lying there on the ground that shot him. Surer than hell. Shot him dead. Look at him. Lock him up.' I said, 'Lady, where is the gun?' Goddam, I'm getting bullshit now, with everybody screaming. The other lady, who is now standing over the two guys, says, 'That muhfuckin' bitch right there took those guns in her house.' About this time another cruiser pulls up, and two of them jump out. 'What you got, Hogan?' 'I got two people shot,' I said, 'I got two fucking guns I can't find, and I got one asshole telling me the guns are in the other's house, and she says the other one's got them.'

"Then the sergeant's cruiser pulls up with two ambulances and a wagon. By this time we have forty or fifty people about. Cars are stopping *now* because they can't get past the cruisers. And there's ten or twelve policemen around looking for the guns. Now one of the ladies starts yelling at the other, 'I'm gonna beat your fuckin' ass, woman,' and the other lady yells back, 'You ain't gonna beat nobody's ass. I'm gonna beat *your* ass.' So she runs up and gets in her house. In the meantime lady number one goes into her house and gets a meat cleaver, only I don't see it because she has it behind her back. 'You take one more step,' lady number two says to lady number one, 'and I'll blow your muhfuckin' head off.' So she's just given me a clue. I say, 'You got a gun, lady?' 'I ain't got me no gun, but I got me a iron, and I'm gonna kill her dead.' Holy Jesus Christ.

"So up the walk comes lady number one. I say, 'Stay right there, lady, you're not coming in.' 'Out of my way, policeman,' she says, and with that she starts walking up the stairs, and I push her back. Up comes the meat cleaver. She's trying to get at the other woman, not me. I grab her around the neck—she's a big, heavy woman—and down the steps we went. I land on my back, and she lands on top of me. I don't know if they ever did get the guns.

"Anyway, my wife was unhappy in the city, and I was getting sick of it, too, after three years, and we had kids to think of. So I resigned and came to Wellfleet. It's not really that different. Just about every call I got in Washington I've had here. The only difference is the tone. In D.C. they say—the guy's real low-key, like he's bored, you know, heard it all before—he says, 'Scout One-three-four and One-two-seven, you have a B and E in progress at Twenty-three-twenty-four Washington Avenue, at the liquor store.' In Wellfleet they say, *'Charlie One, I think there's a B and E going on! Some lady just called me and, ah, ah, there's people going in the back window! And the Johnsons who live next door where the apple cart used to be say they're inside now! Do you want me to call the state police?'*

"I remember one time not that long after I'd been here, me and Gary got a call—'There's a car throwing beer cans all over the road.' We got a description, and we see it, and we get behind it. There's five guys in the car—three in the front and two in the back—and there's beer cans all over the back seat. 'Where you guys going?' I said. 'Aw, we're just driving around the Cape.' He gives me his license and no registration. 'This is my mother's car,' he says. 'Okay, where's the reg?' Nobody else is saying a word. Now that's a tipoff, if they don't even look at you. So the dispatcher calls back on the radio. I had asked her to check on the license plate, and she says the car is stolen. Automatic attitude change. I go back to the car and say, 'This thing's stolen. Get out of the car.' So the driver gets out, and I have his hands on the hood. I have my gun out. Did that as soon as it came back stolen. I'm not pointing it at anybody, just holding it at my side while I'm saying, 'I want you out of the car, and I want *you* on the backside of the car, and I want *you* on the other side.' So they all get out of the car and automatically they start with, 'Did you steal this car, you fucking nut? You didn't tell us.' The car'd been stolen for a month and they're going through this now. We cram all five in the back seat of the cruiser, three sitting and two in their laps. We couldn't cuff anyone because there weren't enough cuffs to go around.

"Off we go to Orleans. And meanwhile Orleans had grabbed three people for disorderly conduct, so there's three prisoners from Orleans, four cops from Orleans, five prisoners from Wellfleet, two cops from Wellfleet, the desk sergeant, the dispatcher, and the Eastham cruiser that backed us up. So there's about twenty people roaming around. The Orleans sergeant comes over and he says, 'Everybody give me your guns, too many free hands here.' So we put the guns in the closet in the typing room.

"I go in there, and I'm sitting down typing and starting to get some order to all this for my report, and all of a sudden Gary comes in and he says, 'One of our prisoners just walked out the door.' The Orleans sergeant told him. Said, 'You just lost a prisoner, he just walked out the door.' Wonderful. We run out the door and down the street and he says, 'We haven't got any guns.' Jesus. So we run back to the station and grab a couple of pistols. I don't know whether I had mine or not, I just grabbed the first one I came to. We're running out and Gary's throwing me bullets, and I'm trying to run down the lawn and load my gun.

"We lost all kinds of time with that and the kid got away. Went back to the station, and just as we're crossing the street to go back in the door, here comes another kid out of the garage. And he's got his *shoes* with him. After the first guy split they made everyone take off his shoes, but this guy must have got his back, or taken someone else's. So I said to Gary, 'Is that one of them?' and he says, 'Yeah, son of a bitch!' and off we go again. And right behind this guy comes Sergeant Fitzpatrick yelling, 'Grab him, grab that fucking nut!'

"I'm getting bullshit now. I'm running down the street after this kid hollering, '*You better stop, you fucking bum. Stop or I'll shoot!*' And Fitzy thought I was going to shoot him. He's yelling, '*You can't shoot him! Don't shoot him! Jesus, Hogan, don't!*' I said, 'I'm not going to shoot him,' and I come up over the ridge and fell flat on my butt, boom, skidding down into the briars, and tore my pants all up, and I hit the tree, and I look up and see this kid running like a fucking deer. It's hotter than hell, did I say that? August, and I haven't caught my breath *lately*. I'm walking around panting. I'll kill him.

"So Gary and I are walking down the road, and I hear the bushes. I whisper to Gary, 'He's in the bushes.' Gary's fucking dying in the heat and all this running around. Fitzy's scratching through the briars, and Gary's got his gun out, and he creeps up and yells, '*Get out here, you fucking asshole!*' And here comes this little kid about seven years old crawling out of the bushes and he says, 'What's going on?' and Gary's going, 'Holy Jesus.' He damn near shot the kid. We go on tromping down the street and we come up to another kid who's about ten. I'll never forget it. Here comes the Orleans cruiser driving by, siren going, and we're saying, 'I don't know where he is,' shrugging our shoulders. This kid's in the driveway, and he points over his shoulder, real cool, like, no shit, and we give him a big wink. I'm dragging my ass up there to this little barn in back of a house. We're *trying* to sneak up, but we're panting and making all kinds of noise. I go up to it and Gary goes around the side. I walk in and look around, there's a hayloft and rakes and whatnot. 'He's not here,' I said.

Made believe I was going back into the woods and Gary's off somewhere. Well, the kid thinks the coast is clear, and he starts climbing down the ladder, and I jump around and grab him. Gary was on the other side of the barn, and he sees the kid through a window coming down the ladder, but he didn't know that I had put the lock on him already. He comes charging like a bull through the woods. The kid is leaning with his hands up against the wall, and Gary comes tromping through. *'Put them up, you son of a bitch, or I'll blow your fucking head off!'* And he's pointing the gun at *me* because I had leaned in to cuff the kid. *'Jesus,* Gary, put it *down,'* I said. We scooped him up and brought him back to the jail. They found the other kid in town waiting for the bus. The lady whose car was stolen didn't even want to press charges. Jesus Christ.

"This job is wonderful, though. For one thing, it's always challenging. It asks a lot from you. It gives me a lot of pride when there's a situation totally out of control, whatever that situation might be, a domestic problem, a fight or an argument, *any* situation, and to get called there and within a certain amount of time to have the people calmed down and all of them waiting for you to give the next word: 'This is what's going to happen, and you're both going to have to calm down.' Half the time a cop doesn't have to say anything. He just walks in and that's it.

"If a person becomes a cop because he likes this power, and there are those, they're going to find out pretty quick that the authority they have is awesome. When society gives a man a gun, and they set up these rules and they say,

'If this happens, or if this happens, you can kill him,' that's an awesome, awesome authority and power.

"Now, you will find cops who are brutal, who abuse it and who will knock people around, but I don't think it's because of the authority. It's because they've become hardened to it. Or they may have got hurt before, and they're not going to let it happen again. There are lots of immature cops when they start—I was immature when I started—and I had an entirely different concept of what policing was about. I didn't think police got hurt. When I say 'hurt,' I mean I knew they got shot dead, but I couldn't conceivably see anyone hitting me. It didn't take too long to get knocked around, though, and you don't like that to happen too often.

"If you're going to get knocked around, even if you're going to *die* as a cop, if you're going to be murdered in the street, you would *like* to have it happen to you saving someone's life, preventing a suicide, or something like that. It makes you feel that you're being used if you get hurt by a jerk who doesn't care what happens to you or whether you have a wife and kids. And it's the same jerk that you pick up every week or every Friday that you have to take to jail. He's the one that's going to hurt you. If I was to get hurt, even badly, doing my job, or doing what I think a policeman ought to do, it wouldn't bother me. Sure, the pain and everything else would, but I would say it was worth it. But to stop some drunk from smacking his wife, and she's going to smack him back, and tomorrow they're going to forget all about it, to get right in the middle of that, and get beat up for them, that's not worth it.

"The advantage is it's always different. People call the station demanding to know why it's snowing. They call up and demand to know the conditions of the roads. They call up because they hear gurgling sounds in their toilets, I've had that happen. They want to know why they are sick, why the weather has changed the way it has. One time I had a car go by, and there was a tree burning in the back. I have no doubt that if I wasn't in uniform that car wouldn't have gone by with a tree burning. You're never going to see the same thing in this job. Sometimes you hope to Christ you never see it again. Your job has to be to handle a problem, no matter what it is, anything at all, you have to be able to handle it for those people who call up and want to know why the weather has changed. Tell them God made it change."

19.

I HAD A .38, Smith & Wesson. It was a moderate-sized gun, with a blue-black bore, a wooden cross-hatched grip, and rust here and there along the handle. I have no idea how old it was—except that it was not by any means new—or how many people had used it before me, or how long it had sat unused in the bottom drawer of the chief's desk. It had a row of notches along the handle, six or seven, I forget now how many, but I don't know what they were from. I know that Sherman had once used my gun but had got rid of it because it was in such bad shape that he considered it useless. Paul told me to be careful with it because he had known it to jam. I didn't know what jam meant, and I still don't, but I assumed it meant backfire, so whenever I had the gun out I held it to the side.

I never learned to fire it properly. Holding it to the side, I couldn't aim it well and had to estimate. The smallest target I ever hit was the side of a hill.

I had two episodes of instruction with my gun, both brief and happening months after it had been given to me. The first took place in Provincetown, where I went to see a training film called *Shoot—DON'T Shoot*. The film depicted a number of scenes—among others, a traffic stop, a robbery, a burglary, an assault, and a rape—presented as if the camera were your eyes. As it began, the Provincetown police chief handed out a gun loaded with blanks, and the idea was to decide whether to use the gun against the person facing you on the screen. The gun was passed from one person to another, each of them having a turn at using or not using it.

The choice had to be made quickly, and it was hard to be sure of yourself. You had to take into account the number of people around and whether they would be hurt if you shot; also, whether the man or woman with the weapon meant absolutely to use it. Even if it was used, there was the problem of timing. For instance, if a man had a knife and quickly cocked his arm to throw it, but then in the same motion dropped it, you were wrong if you shot, although it would have been perfectly sensible to assume that by cocking his arm he intended to throw the knife at you. And if he threw the knife and you shot at the moment it left his fingers, you were also wrong because you shot an unarmed man. You could only rightfully shoot in self-defense during the several hundredths of a second between the moment his arm started forward and the instant of release. So far as I know, no one can think and react in that short an interval. Furthermore, the people on the screen reached into pockets and sometimes pulled out guns and sometimes didn't. Whatever they pulled out was concealed until the very last second. One man standing in shadow unexpectedly drew something shiny from his breast pocket and held it toward the camera and was shot by somebody in the audience before any of us could see it was a police badge.

I sat through seven or eight scenes and guessed right about as often as the people around me—cops from Truro and Provincetown—which was roughly half the time. Sometimes the audience members shot when they shouldn't have, and sometimes they failed to shoot when it was necessary. When it came my turn the images on the screen were in full daylight, and it was as if the camera was seeing what I would have seen, slowly walking along a row of storefronts. Ahead, on my left, the glass doors were open to the street. On one was a MasterCharge decal, and on the other a sign for a brand of paint, and a large sign that read "Open." The camera went through the doors, taking me with it. Inside, a Black man in profile to me held a gun on the man at the cash register, who had his hands in the air. Neither of them saw me. A voice on the screen said, "Police, *drop* it!" The man at the cash register fell back safely out of range, and I shot the Black man as he turned toward me with the gun. His shot came after mine. I relaxed. A second Black man stepped from behind the first and fired a shotgun at me. I hadn't seen him.

As I passed the gun to the man next to me, I saw I had gripped it so tightly that the cross-hatching on the butt had left an impression on my palm and the pads of my fingers.

"If you fired only once," the narrator said, "you might as well not have fired at all." So discouraging.

At my second lesson, which was with Joe, I fired my own gun. One evening in the fall he took me out to the sandpit behind the town highway department barns, where there was a small practice range. He loaded my gun with dummy bullets and stood behind me. I fired six shots at an even slow pace, he reloaded, and I fired six quickly into the sand. Disappointment was what I felt more than anything else. Instead of a loud report, the gun made a tinny sound like a small firecracker—it left my ears ringing—and none of the bullets went where I thought I was pointing. It looked like they went wherever the hell they felt like.

Policemen call guns equalizers and Paul used to say, "As long as I have Mr. Smith and Mr. Wesson with me, I'm not afraid of anybody." Although I never fired my gun in the line of duty, or pointed it at anyone, I drew it regularly. Whenever I had to search a dark building I pulled it out. It made me feel better.

One midnight-to-eight in the spring when I was alone, I answered a call for a B & E in progress at a house by the bay. When I got there I took with me the shotgun that was kept in the car for protection. The house was locked and the call seemed to be a false alarm, but while I was around the back I heard a sound in the bushes behind me. I pumped the gun, which dropped a shell into the chamber. This made a lot of noise, and I did it for effect.

The sound in the bushes turned out to be from a cat. I put the gun down and played for a while with the cat and, since it was getting to be dawn, decided to go have breakfast. I put the gun back in its bracket, and after breakfast I went home. As it happened, I had unintentionally left the safety disengaged. Charlie, the next man to use the car, couldn't believe his eyes when sometime during the morning he noticed the gun with the safety off and the shell in its chamber. I suppose if he had hit a bump hard enough, the gun would have blown off a portion of the roof. I was summoned to the station by the chief, and Paul was assigned to show me how the gun worked and to watch while I practiced ejecting unused shells from it.

At some point during the winter I decided to fire the shotgun. I drove into the woods around three in the morning, and walked to a clearing. I didn't want to damage any trees, so I shouldered the gun and pointed it straight down into the ground, but I was extremely reluctant to pull the trigger. When I finally did, there was an explosion, and for an instant the entire woods seemed blue in the flash. There was a hole by my feet, and because I hadn't held the gun properly it had kicked back painfully into my shoulder. I had no more curiosity about it. I put it back in the cruiser, and I don't think I ever took it out again.

No Wellfleet policeman has ever fired his gun in action. I would say the same thing for Truro except that while I was working, a Truro patrolman fired a shot, a warning shot, he insisted, over the heads of some children who were lighting firecrackers. He does not work there anymore, although I think he is still a policeman, in a town near Boston.

One evening when I came in to work I saw a rifle—one of the small collection the department owned to make up a proper-looking honor guard for the Fourth of July parade—lying on a desk outside the chief's office. The dispatcher said Hogan had just shot the sergeant with it, and started laughing. When Hogan stopped in to pick me up, I asked him what the dispatcher had meant.

"Oh, Gary was throwing the shit around," he said, "like he does, you know, 'Jesus Christ, I can't find this,' or something like that, and he storms into the office. So I went in the closet and got the rifle and loaded a blank round into it. Then I went into his office and started something with him, you know, 'You son of a bitch, I can only stand so much of this,' and I pointed it right at him, pulled the trigger and it went *Boom!* He liked to come right off the goddam desk. He went completely white. '*You crazy son of a bitch,*' he said. He turned around to see if I put a hole in the wall."

One afternoon, Chickie and I were in the station having lunch, and two of the dispatchers were there also. We were talking about guns, and I reached for mine to take a look at it. I was leaning back in my chair and didn't manage a very good grip, and I dropped the gun. I bent over for it, and sat up ready to rejoin the conversation, but there was nobody else there.

"Where'd everybody go?" I said.

One of the dispatchers looked around from behind a desk, and the other one peered over the top of the counter. Chickie was in a closet, and when he came out he said, "Hire the handicapped."

During the summer the Wellfleet police challenged the park rangers who work for the National Seashore to a shooting competition. I think Paul organized it. I was not told about it until afterward, for fear that I might have showed up. The rangers proved expert shots, and even without me the Wellfleet police got a drubbing.

One afternoon, fishing around in a closet, I found an instruction sheet for my gun. It had directions on how to clean it and take it apart, and a reproduction of an exquisite graphite drawing of the gun, with arrows labeling the parts: barrel pins, stirrup pins, hammer nose rivets, bolt plungers, hand-spring torsion pins, strain screws, sear springs, rebound slide and cylinder stop springs, escutcheons, extractors, extractor rod collars, magna stocks, gas rings, hands, and cylinder stop studs.

Sometimes when I was a passenger in the cruiser, the man driving would head the car to the town line and we would meet a cruiser from Truro or Eastham. Occasionally there was business involved, the transfer of papers or a prisoner, or some kind of information, but usually there wasn't and they would talk and pass the time—the score of the baseball game, some problem they were having, gossip they had heard about someone they knew in common, or something about guns: their finish, their power, or the way they had had the trigger springs in their favorite pistols replaced with finer ones and the triggers shaved to improve the action. I would have liked to join in, but most of the time I did not know what they were talking about and had nothing to add from my experience.

One night I was in the car with Joe and we were talking with a patrolman from Eastham. He was showing us his new gun. It was large and heavy and had nickel-plating shiny as chrome. Joe asked him where he got it and the patrolman said that over the summer he had ticketed one of the executives of Smith & Wesson for speeding. The case had just come to trial, and in appreciation for his having arranged to have it continued without a finding, the executive got him the gun at half price.

Most of the others owned their guns. They preferred .357 magnums, which are big and exceptionally powerful. One night I fired five shots from Chickie's .357. Flames spit from the barrel and the chamber. You had to hold the gun in a certain way so that the flashes from the chamber didn't burn your finger.

As far as I can remember, Joe and I were the only ones who had department .38's. Joe told me that in Washington the force hadn't allowed its officers to carry anything more powerful than a .38, and especially not .357's. He said, "The problem is with a thirty-eight you've got your soft-nosed ammunition, where if I am pointing at you, and I *hit* you, the bullet will stay with you and drop you. Supposedly. Sometimes you may have to fire more than once. A three-fifty-seven, though, will send a bullet through the person you're aiming at, through the guy behind *him*, and into the guy behind him. It may stop there or it might go into another guy. Can't tell. If you want to, you can shoot through an engine block with a three-fifty-seven. Like I say, they didn't use them in D.C., but then the fact there is they had a department of fifty-one hundred psychotics and they couldn't possibly issue us anything but the minimum weapon."

As a result of a call we handled together, Joe decided to get a new gun. We had been told that there was an injured seagull wandering in the road near the center of town. It was illegal to shoot seagulls, but this one had already been shot and couldn't have recovered. It was standing in the center of the road when we arrived, but when we got out of the car, it started walking off for the woods, dragging one wing, and Joe followed it. I heard a shot, and after a moment another. A pause again, and then another. In all there were five. Joe came back out of the woods studying the gun in his hand and shaking his head. "Five shots," he said. "I kept hitting it and it would stagger around a moment, not even fall *down*, mind you, and traipse off again. I want a *magnum*."

Paul carried a gun with him all the time, because he believed a policeman should. At a department meeting he proposed making this mandatory. "You could be buying milk in Cumberland Farms," he said, "and some guy comes in and sticks up the place. What's going to happen when some lady turns around and says, 'You're a cop, do something.' The guy's going to turn right around and smoke you, and you won't be able to do anything about it because you don't have your gun." The chief didn't think a rule was necessary, and instead left it up to each officer. Off-duty, Paul wore his gun on a sleek holster that clipped to his waist and couldn't be detected even under a t-shirt.

He once told me, "After all the fifty or however many guns it is I've owned, I settled on the forty-five. It's not a powerful velocitywise as, say, a thirty-eight, but in a thirty-eight you're shooting a hundred-and-twenty-five grain bullet, compared to the two-hundred-and-thirty-grain one I use in a forty-five. It's like taking a tack hammer and hitting something with it, compared to a ball-peen. They use an example of a safe door closing: it moves slow, but when it hits, it's all over. A forty-five I can carry on or off duty, it fits right on my hip; plus it shoots better in the respect that you don't have a recoil—you can get back down on your target again.

"And the ideal thing of it is, at least from what my readings were on guns, your forty-five was ninety-five percent knockdown power. In other words, one shot, a good torso hit, ninety-five percent of the time you're going to knock the guy down, he won't get up anymore. Otherwise, you're wasting your time, you wound the guy but you don't knock him down. He can still shoot you, if he's got a gun, and he does have or you wouldn't have shot in the first place. With a thirty-eight you're talking fifty percent knockdown, and with a three-fifty-seven the thing of it is you're apt to take out citizens too. With this, ninety-five percent of the time it's just one shot. One bullet hole. And that looks a whole lot better in court than having six bullet holes. You got six and the judge is going to say, 'Jesus Christ, you think you stopped him long enough?'"

It never bothered me that I didn't know anything about my gun. The truth is, I never thought about it. It took me a few weeks to accustom myself to its weight on my hip, and then I forgot about it. I was never comfortable having it at home, though. I wanted to leave it at the station, but the sergeant would not allow it. He told me I might need it sometime on my way to or from work. I might get ambushed, he said.

I used to unload my gun after work and hide the bullets in my desk, or in a blanket in the closet, or under the bed, or in back of a book on the shelf, and the gun behind the washing machine in the basement or under a toolbox in the workshop. (Charlie's wife told me that after he unloaded his gun he often locked it with his handcuffs around the pipes under the bathroom sink.) But I could not relax with the gun around.

One night I sat on the edge of my bed and put the gun to my temple and wondered what makes people actually pull the trigger. It scared the hell out of me.

I was glad when the year was up. I felt I'd survived something. I never cared for the things I had to concern myself with—warnings, tickets, arrests, confrontations, problems. For the most part they were small-minded. It was depressing to be disliked by people I didn't even know, depressing to be cursed in public and to work midnight-to-eights over and over, depressing to harass the kids on Main Street only because the selectmen wanted it done. Occasionally someone I knew would invite me over to play guitars, but it was usually awkward because there were always other people around who had dropped by to hear the music and smoke dope, and while I didn't know them, they knew me by sight as a policeman and couldn't decide if I was undercover or what. It made me very self-conscious.

There were parts, though, and there were people. Billy, Joe, and Paul especially.

And the wife of a friend of Joe's, who invited us into her trailer one afternoon and served us chocolate cake and Coca-Cola, in the midst of three children who were playing happily on the kitchen floor with spoons and a coffee cup.

A Canadian and his wife who liked a restaurant I had recommended and came back to see me on Main Street and insisted I accept a six-pack of beer, which I had to hide behind the Lighthouse until I could pick it up after work.

The woods, of course, and the water, and the broad clear sky at night over the water, and riding around.

Watching the fishing fleet leave the harbor in the dark before dawn.

A man at the pier, sunburned and drunk from an afternoon on the bay, who flagged me down in the cruiser by yelling "Taxi" and had me use his camera to take his picture with a big striped bass he had caught.

A contentious sour old man who gave me a cup of tea one afternoon when I went to his house to deliver a message and confused me (I suppose he was senile) with Billy Brooks and said, "Sit, Billy, sit down. You know, Billy, I knew your mother. A fine woman. A fine, fine woman. Why, I guess I've known you, Billy, since the day you were born."

The night Billy and I drove around in the cruiser laughing so hard we had to park the car, for no reason except pleasure over a dumb joke.

The image of Billy, harassed beyond endurance by a group of forty or fifty kids on Halloween, stepping from his car into the chill October night screaming, "Get the school bus!"

Billy's saying one night, "I used to be shy, but then about eighteen I decided I was going to break out of it."

Having coffee one morning in town with the chief and feeling cool at being seen with him.

The Christmas Eve I spent at Joe's drinking beer and supermarket egg-nog with him and his wife and another friend and talking and Joe telling stories.

The care Joe took in seeing I was as prepared as he could make me.

And the trust I put in all of them.

Even so, it was an immense relief to me when at the end of my last night of work I drove down to the ocean, walked to the edge of the water, pulled out my gun, and emptied it into the waves.

Afterword

I AM NO longer that young man. I can close my eyes and
see him, I can hear him say things, but he exists in his
own time and in some sense without me. I'm not even
sure I ever was him. He is a re-creation of a kind. Layers
of memory are involved, since what I wrote was what I
recalled. I ought to have kept notes but I didn't, except
very intermittently. I felt that if something was worth
writing about, I would remember it. "Alec," William Maxwell wrote to me, "look at Wellfleet in your *mind* and the
words will attach themselves to what you see."

I was a policeman for a year, and I wrote about it for
three years. It took so long because I didn't know what I
was doing, and also because I was very impressionable. I
tended to write in the style of whatever book I was reading. When I was reading *As I Lay Dying*, I sounded like
Faulkner, and when I was reading *A Farewell to Arms*, I

sounded like Hemingway. I sounded like Isak Dinesen while reading *Out of Africa* and like Gertrude Stein while reading *The Autobiography of Alice B. Toklas*. I was a species of prose ventriloquist. For a time, I thought that the words I was using were too simple to be writing, so I started using bigger, more literary words; one of them was *crepuscular*, which I had encountered in Henry James. The next time I saw Maxwell he said, "It sounds like you swallowed a dictionary."

Sometime during my second year of working on *Midnights*, the Provincetown *Advocate* did a story about me and the book, and the sister of an editor in New York read it and sent it to her brother, and he wrote me and asked to see the book when it was finished. I sent it to him, and he took nine months to tell me that he didn't want to publish it. My parents had a guest house on their property, and one summer it was rented by a reporter for the *New York Times*, and he read the first chapter of my book and sent it to his publisher, and the publisher wrote back, "I cannot encourage this young man enough to abandon this book." One day outside the library in Wellfleet I saw a stray piece of paper at my feet, and I picked it up. On the stationery of a literary journal I had heard of, an editor had written, "Feel free to submit more of your work, but please be aware that there are enough of us here for whom your writing does nothing that it probably isn't sensible." When I was discouraged, Maxwell used to say, "There are a lot of other ways to make a living . . ." I was sustained by the belief that I was the only person in America writing a book about being a policeman in a small town. So far as I knew, there weren't any other books on the subject, except maybe ones that were fiction. I never asked myself whether my book was good. I put all my faith in its novelty.

An editor at *The Atlantic* declined to publish an excerpt but not without first condescending to me. The magazine *Yankee* declined, too. I submitted the book to the *Cape Codder*, a weekly newspaper, hoping they might serialize it over the summer, and they took a few months to say no, adding that they might be willing to look at it again if I found a good editor, which I thought was rich. A few more publishers in New York whose addresses I had looked up in the phone book also passed. The last was a firm that specialized in books with travel-related themes, where I had thought I had a shot. What finally happened is a friend called one day and told me he had rented his house to a writer from *The New Yorker* and that I should meet him. The writer was George W. S. Trow. We became friends, and after a few months he said I needed an agent, and he got me one, Elaine Markson, whose office was on the second floor of a walkup in the Village. She sent my book to Joe Fox, Truman Capote's editor at Random House. By then I was living in New York, and Fox took me to a fancy lunch and said that if I would change this and that, he would look at the manuscript again. I changed everything he wanted me to change, and instead of receiving another rejection, I got a contract and a check for five thousand dollars. Six years had passed since my first night in the police car and Paul saying, "So murder could have happened here—and we don't know about it."

THE YOUNG MAN who wrote this book has no idea what will happen to him, where he will live or what he will do, whether he will embrace life or be defeated by it, and I know what happened, for the next forty years, anyway. What I like best about him is the company he kept. The eight other men knew things about the larger world that I didn't know, even if the larger world was defined mostly by the borders of the town they patrolled. They had been soldiers, some of them; they had suffered disappointments; most of them were married and some had children. They carried themselves with a confidence that I could only impersonate. In the years since, their characters have only deepened for me. I regard myself as fortunate for having landed among them, for their patience and kindness toward me.

I must have looked to them like a silly proposition— skinny, small, naive, unskilled, unreliable, unprepared, of questionable judgment, prone to mistakes, comically inept, so different from them as to be almost exotic, and proven to be of very little use when matters turned serious. I was lucky I never got hurt. I had a child's belief that no one would harm a policeman, and it made me brave in a playacting way and protected me like a magic spell.

On practically every occasion when I have had the opportunity in a piece of writing I have mentioned that I was a policeman in Wellfleet, because I am proud of having had such an adventure. Nothing I've done has changed me as much as that year changed me. Beforehand, my life had been passed among people who thought more or less the same way that I did, and since then my life has been passed that way, too. It is as if I had spent a year as a recruit in some faraway place and returned having seen strange things and with impressions that still retain the power to instruct me.

IN REREADING THE book for the first time in many years, I see that another of the gifts I was given as a writer was to find myself in the company of natural-born storytellers, Joe and Paul especially. From the template their talk provided, I began to seek out people who have a talent for finding the right words to frame a thought or an experience or a feeling. I learned the pleasure in hearing what people want to tell you and that many people have waited a long time for someone to listen to them.

I wish I hadn't arrested the selectman's son. I wish I had waited for the others to arrive and help me decide what to do. I see, uncomfortably, that in writing about the experience, I still felt indignant, and you are entitled to know why. The consequence of my action was that the sergeant, Paul, Chickie, Joe, and the chief all lost their jobs, not all at the same time and not all for the same reasons, but because of what I did and unjustly and as a means of revenge. I still feel angry when I think of how they were treated, but it is like watching a play; I can't change any of it.

Elaine Markson is dead. Joe Fox is dead. George Trow is dead, and William Maxwell is dead, too. When Maxwell and I started working together, he was roughly the age that I am now. I loved him, and am still not over his dying, despite its being almost twenty years ago. Even though he was ninety-one, I wasn't prepared for it.

The selectman is dead. The selectman's son is dead. Also, the chief, the sergeant, and Chickie. I haven't seen the others in many years, but I would like to.

Alec Wilkinson,

2022

A NOTE ON THE TYPE

Midnights has been set in Caslon. This modern version is based on the early-eighteenth-century roman designs of British printer William Caslon I, whose typefaces were so popular that they were employed for the first setting of the Declaration of Independence, in 1776. Eric Gill's humanist typeface Gill Sans, from 1928, has been used for display.

Book Design & Composition by Tammy Ackerman